CHRISTIAN HEALING

G000068639

CHRISTIAN HEALING

WHAT CAN WE BELIEVE?

—

Edited by Ernest Lucas

LYNX

First published in Great Britain 1997
Lynx Communications
Society for Promoting Christian Knowledge
Holy Trinity Church
Marylebone Road
London NW1 4DU

British Library Cataloguing-in-Publication Data

A catalogue record of this book is available from the British Library

ISBN 1–901443–00–0

Typeset by Bibliocraft, Dundee
Printed in Great Britain by Biddles Ltd, Guildford and King's Lynn

Contents

———

Acknowledgements

The author and publishers would like to thank the Revd Christopher Hamel Cooke for permission to reproduce his sample form of liturgy for a healing service and the Very Revd John F. Petty for permission to reproduce the pattern for a non-liturgical healing service (both in chapter 2, Practical Appendix).

The poem 'Kate' (chapter 7) is reproduced by kind permission of Hodder & Stoughton.

Introduction

Health and healing are major concerns for most people. Governments spend a sizeable proportion of their tax revenues on health services for their citizens. Major multi-national companies make large profits out of drugs and medical equipment. Wealthy individuals spend large sums of money on private medical care of various kinds. It may well be that the growth in concern about health and fitness that has occurred in western countries in the last several decades is related in part to a decline in religious belief. This may have increased the fear of death, so that it must be postponed as long as possible by all means possible. It may also have prompted people to invest more in trying to make this life as perfect as possible (heaven on earth, since they have lost the hope of a future heaven).

Christians have long had an interest in health and healing, and have played a major role in the development of medical care.[1] This flows from the fact that healing played an important part in the ministry of Jesus Christ and in the early days of the Christian Church. There has been a renewal of interest in the 'ministry of healing' (however that may be understood) in Christian churches in the past few decades. The cynic may see this as the Church simply following the trends in society at large. A more charitable view would be that the Church is responding to the felt needs of the society in which it is set – which is an understandable and worthwhile thing to do. It may even be that the trends in society have led Christians to re-examine the roots of their faith and practice and revitalize something that had been at least partially lost.

Whatever the reason for the revival of interest in healing among Christians, the fact is that it has become a matter of debate, and sometimes division, within churches. In 1991 the Margaret Houghton Memorial Trust decided to bring together a group of Christian health-care professionals, pastoral workers, theologians and ethicists to discuss the Church's healing ministry. Those invited were chosen because they came from different traditions of Christian healing ministry and were known to hold differing

1

understandings and views about such a ministry. The group, of about twenty-four people, first met at Southwell House in London on 1 and 2 November 1991. They discussed some papers which had been prepared and circulated in advance. These had the aim of helping them map out the areas of agreement and disagreement. All were surprised at how wide the areas of agreement were once one got behind the rhetoric of the different positions. They agreed to embark on a process of consultations aimed at discussing some areas of disagreement in more depth.

Three further meetings followed, on 30 and 31 October 1992, 5 and 6 November 1993 and 10 December 1994. Once again, these were based on papers which were prepared and circulated in advance. Initially each paper was in two parts: a position statement and a response. The two writers were usually a medical practitioner and someone with theological expertise. After each consultation the pairs of writers rewrote their papers and interpreted them in the light of the discussion of them. This involved meeting in small groups between the main consultations.

Nearly everyone who took part in the consultations found the process a very valuable, even exciting, process. We are glad that the revised papers are being published so that others can gain some of the benefit we received from the consultations. It must be emphasized that the papers represent *only the views of their authors*. Although they take into account the comments made in the discussion of the papers, they do not necessarily represent the views of the participants in the consultations. In every paper, some views are expressed, or positions advocated, with which some of the participants would disagree to a greater or lesser extent.

Appendix 1 consists of a 'consensus statement'. It was initially drawn up by Sir John Houghton. He and his wife Sheila acted as host and hostess at the consultations, and Sir John chaired the plenary discussions. The statement was developed during the course of the consultation, its main purpose being to assist in the clarification, the consolidation and the recording of the main points which arose. It is included in the book because it might well be a good starting point for other discussions of the Church's ministry of healing.

Appendix 2 is a list of all those who took part in the consultation process. Some who attended the initial meeting were unable to commit themselves to the full consultation process. A few were invited to join during the process when the need for additional expertise became apparent.

The book begins with two chapters which take as their starting point what is actually being done by Christians in terms of healing ministry. The first combines an account of the experience of a missionary doctor with a theological reflection on this experience which seeks to understand how God is at work bringing about healing in this world which Christians believe is God's creation. This is followed by an evaluation of various kinds of church-based healing ministry. These two chapters raise a number of issues concerning what we understand by health and healing. This is the subject of Chapter 3. They also raise points concerning how Christians understand and evaluate the implications of Jesus' ministry. Chapter 4 deals with this.

The desire to heal, and to be healed, arises because of the suffering which illness causes. The existence of suffering in a world created by a good and loving God has always been a major problem for Christian believers and, indeed, for people of other faiths too. Chapter 5 combines a theological discussion of this problem with insights into the practical pastoral care of those who are suffering.

For a variety of reasons, mental health has always been a more problematic area for Christians than has physical health. The reasons for this are considered in Chapter 6 and this leads into a wider discussion of mental health care from a Christian perspective.

The one thing we can all be sure of in this life is death. Ageing and dying are the subject of our last chapter. Both present a challenge which must be met by any Christian understanding of health and healing. Is ageing an 'illness' we should seek to cure? How can a healing ministry take the fact of death into account? For many people the fear of death is closely related to the fear that it may come about only after a long and painful illness. Christians have played a major part in the development of the hospice movement, which helps people to 'die well'. It has been responsible for major advances in the control of pain. Just as important is the lead it has given in meeting the social and spiritual aspects of the needs of the dying and their loved ones.

The chapters differ in style and format. This reflects both the preferences of the authors and the nature of their subject. The variety adds interest to the reading of the book.

The Margaret Houghton Memorial Trust, which sponsored the consultations, was set up by her relatives and friends in memory of a medical doctor who worked in community health in Oxford, England, and who died in 1986 after a long battle with cancer. It reflects Dr Margaret Houghton's own concern to improve the mutual understanding and cooperation between health-care professionals and Christian ministers in the care of the unwell, the dying and the bereaved and their families. Two theological colleges in Oxford, Regent's Park (Baptist) and Wycliffe Hall (Church of England), are represented on the Trust. The Institute for Contemporary Christianity in London acts as the executive agency of the Trust. We are grateful to the Trust for sponsoring this publication.

References

1. See *The Influence of Christians in Medicine* (The Christian Medical Fellowship 1984) and *Heralds of Health* (The Christian Medical Fellowship 1985).

CHAPTER 1

How Are People Healed Today? The Relationship Between the 'Medical' and the 'Spiritual' in Healing

—

Dr Bill Lees
Revd Dr Paul Fiddes

A Christian understanding of the world has to bring together our experience of life, with all its complexity and messiness, and our understanding of what the Bible teaches, with all the uncertainties that might arise as we try to interpret correctly things that were written many centuries ago in a culture very different from ours. In this chapter a recently retired doctor who worked in community medicine in Reading, and before that worked for eighteen years as a doctor and church-planter in South East Asia with the Borneo Evangelical Mission, describes some of his experience of life as someone concerned to bring people healing. A theologian who teaches Christian Doctrine at Regent's Park College in the University of Oxford gives his reflections on these experiences as he tries to understand them in the light of the Bible.

Facing the Unknown: A Doctor's View

Christian doctors see all healing as God's healing, a view which contrasts with that of the majority in the profession, who have a secular outlook. All doctors would agree, however, that in the final analysis the most we can do is to help or encourage the natural healing process. Often we need to do nothing other than monitor the spontaneous resolution of the disease condition. Ambroise Pare in the sixteenth century said it well, 'I dressed the wound, but God healed him.'

As a profession we are excited by the progress of research and the greatly increased depth of understanding of the body's response to a wide variety of problems. But sometimes we feel remarkably helpless and have to admit to large areas of ignorance.

As we consider the medical approach to healing at the end of the twentieth century, we face a very different scene from that of our predecessors at the end of the nineteenth century. General health, at least in the prosperous and privileged western world, is so much better. Previously mysterious conditions, like Hodgkins' Disease, are now understood and yield to treatment. Vicious viral diseases like smallpox have been virtually eliminated. Bacterial infections, such as pneumonia in the very young and very old, are now less common and when they do occur, are dramatically curtailed by contemporary antibiotics. There have been massive reductions in infant and child death rates and an increased expectation of life.

There have been huge advances, not least in surgery with the development of transplant and replacement techniques. But we also have to admit we face limits to our medical technology. The changes have not all been in one direction; the currently very prevalent angina and coronary heart disease were rare 100 years ago and there is more than a hint that the prosperity we enjoy (involving a rich diet, highly refined food and stress) are in part responsible. Suppressed immunity to certain strains of virus has appeared. We must also register, with all humility, a different kind of limit; many of the great advances that have been made in general health are not due to the direct application of medicine but to the improvement of public health in areas of clean water, hygiene and nutrition.

Even more fundamentally, I want to suggest, the basic problem of our understanding of healing has not changed. We still have to find an understanding of the situation in which two people in apparently identical positions respond differently. Why is it that one becomes ill and the other does not? Or two people become ill, and although both are equally vigorous, one recovers and the other dies; why is this? Or again, there may be two young men in similar general health, and the one who spends significantly *less* time surfing and in the sun gets a melanoma (a form of skin cancer).

As a student, I remember the excitement of discovering 'exactly' why I had a spot on my face – a bacterial infection of the skin pore! The answer, when you know it, is so simple. But it soon dawned on me that there were many other pores equally exposed to the same bacteria, and on the same face, that were mercifully not developing into uncomfortable lesions. The conditions in all areas were essentially identical in terms of infection levels, and the various defence mechanisms of the body. Why the spot? Why the spot where it was and not somewhere else? I was so disappointed to realize that my new learning, that at first appeared as a complete and splendidly satisfactory answer, in fact left me with the old question unanswered.

The same question faces us as we follow through a disease process from its unseen beginnings to its fatal outcome. Cancer of the stomach, symptom-free for so long, is a pathological process we are increasingly familiar with. Surgeons tell us of opening an abdomen for radical surgery only to find widespread secondaries. Although the earlier diagnosis had seemed to be absolutely clear, the surgical plan now has to be abandoned and the abdomen closed. The outlook is a life expectancy of a few weeks rather than a few months. Yet for all this, more than one surgeon has been amazed to have the same patient come back ten years later but with an entirely different problem!

A brain tumour in children, called a neuroblastoma, is notoriously difficult to treat particularly in the first twelve months of life. However it is recognized that a not insignificant number spontaneously regress. Why? We do not know. So while our medical knowledge has advanced at a rapidly increasing pace and we have found more answers in recent years, this is only to find that new answers raise new questions, or rather push the old questions further back.

Empirical Strategies in the Face of the Unknown

The ancient world worked 'empirically' to find answers by trial and error, but still had little idea as to *why* they worked. Bird's dung in the eye sounds an unlikely way of helping the healing process. The twentieth-century analysis of 2,000-year-old empirical knowledge demonstrates that belladonna is present in appreciable quantities in the dung of certain birds. Clearly the birds that ate the right berries had been chosen. Today we use exactly the same active ingredient.

To take another example, the contemporary medical world is linked with a coat of arms that depicts serpents. This goes back to the Greco-Roman god of medicine, Asklepios/Aesculapius. A recent article in *The Lancet* speaks of two non-poisonous snakes found in Greece and Italy. The Italian authors report that an inscription found in Epidauros tells about the healing of a 'sore in his toe'; it relates that 'The snake healed the toe with its tongue.' The research of the modern doctors found that the epidermal growth factor was present in the oral and perioral tissue of the snakes. Perhaps our coat of arms witnesses to more about empirical knowledge than we realized.

In fact, our contemporary knowledge is constantly being extended empirically as well as by specifically directed research. Penicillin came to us as a result of an unexpected observation of the inhibition of bacterial growth that certainly was not being 'looked for'. Indeed it could easily have been missed but for an alert Alexander Fleming noting something unusual and immediately asking himself, 'Why?'.

We can ask ourselves what was happening when a young, intelligent consultant surgeon became totally despairing about his daughter's eczema. Desperate scratching and screaming that disturbed neighbours were part of daily life. He and his wife had been to the best paediatricians, skin specialists and allergists without, it would appear, significant relief. In desperation he responded to a report that an elderly Chinese woman in a run-down part of Soho might be able to help. He queued with the rest of the patients and after the consultation was given a herbal mixture that he described as foul smelling and a 'cross between a broth and a gravy'. The long-suffering nine-year-old got the stuff down, and very marked improvement followed. She was soon able to wear a wider range of clothing and live a more normal life. Had the Chinese woman discovered empirically for herself, or learned from her forebears, of a significant treatment that one day may make a pharmaceutical firm rich? A recent television programme about her may have made this more likely.

Not long ago I was speaking with a friend who is a highly respected missionary-doctor, a keen researcher who worked in

Africa with Burkitt on the epidemiology of Burkitt's tumour. He had been suffering with troublesome symptoms for some time, and then found that pain control was no longer being achieved. His GP could find no adequate combination and in desperation, pending the consultant's return from leave, asked if my friend would be willing to try acupuncture which the GP himself would administer. Four needles were placed in the most painful areas on the lateral aspect of his thigh and he was told to leave them for half an hour and then withdraw them. My friend did just that and with a glint of joy in his eyes and a quizzical smile told me the result was remarkable – free from pain for the first time in many days. Is there a lot more about the effects of 'counterirritation' for us to learn?

The Mysterious Physical-Psychological Interface: Pages from a Doctor's Case-Book

Christians lay stress on the wholeness of the human being, so of all groups we are the least surprised by the extent of the interplay of physical, psychological and emotional factors. For years this interaction has been recognized. It is now so firmly accepted that to show the efficacy of a drug it is no longer sufficient to demonstrate that a treatment using it is better than another *treatment*. Instead, the drug must be shown to be better than a *placebo*. That is, a test must be undertaken using a tablet with the active ingredient and an apparently identical tablet without the material under examination, and the test must be administered without the doctor or patient knowing which is which. No-one is surprised to see improvement in *both* groups of patients – that is normal. We have to look for a significantly *better* result with the proposed new drug.

Undoubtedly the mind has an influence over the body which can be dramatic. I recall an anaesthetics teacher telling of a patient who said he would die if he had an anaesthetic. He was duly examined and reassured, firstly that he was not at risk and secondly that the surgery was in his best interests. The patient insisted he would die, which he proceeded to do early in the anaesthetic process.

A medical friend of mine has a colleague who fortunately has time on his side as his practice does not have to generate significant income. He finds as he listens and talks, perhaps for an hour or two with a patient, that his need to resort to medication is enormously

9

reduced. He reports the case of an elderly man who had widespread aches and pains in his leg and ankle. As they talked, major areas of disagreement between husband and wife became very apparent. The three-way conversation facilitated by the doctor went on for one and a half hours. The man 'forgot' his aches and pains and left contentedly without medication.

Another doctor who was establishing a new practice in Shropshire also had time on his side before he built up his list. He reported meeting an elderly woman with severe and painful arthritis in her hands and wrists. The doctor sat down and suggested she told him about herself. She spoke of her perception of being rejected by mother, father, brother, sister, others at school, teachers. After sustained listening, and a brief silent prayer, the GP ventured to ask, 'Is there an element of bitterness in this?'. The woman hesitated and reflected. She conceded that there could be, but asked, 'What can you do about it?'. The meaning of prayer and forgiveness were discussed and then they prayed together. She spoke of feeling better, offered a cup of tea, and when she returned from the kitchen exclaimed in amazement that, without thinking, she had filled the kettle full. For a long time she had only half filled it because she could not lift a full one. Having put the tray down she demonstrated a degree of movement that surprised her. Over the weeks the recovery continued. Was she healed as a result of prayer or because her mind had been freed of its bitterness?

How many of us – in the medical profession – have time or inclination to focus on what is often a hidden agenda when we are presented with an overt problem, and are pushed by the appointment system?

I recall a very prosaic man with a Cambridge PhD. He had suffered a minor but distinctly uncomfortable whiplash injury following a bump from the car behind him. In a church service there was an invitation to come forward for prayer, and he was surprised at himself when he went forward and asked for prayer for his neck. Some weeks later he testified that he was even more surprised, but nevertheless delighted, that the pain had gone. I believe it to be highly significant that he was also full of praise to God that he had been able to forgive the driver who bumped him and caused him the injury, although he had not thought consciously about the need for this when he had requested prayer.

At times, we in the medical profession appear to have a less sharp focus on the emotional and psychological aspects of illness than we ought. Perhaps there is simply a lack of inclination. Or is it because we are preoccupied with the more tangible, measurable and better taught side of medicine? The patients' felt need in this area is high, but they probably have limited expectations of help from the medical profession. Do we thus inadvertently push patients into looking for other answers?

Coping with the Unknown: A Professional Mind-Set

Doctors, as I aim to have shown, are aware of severe limitations in their knowledge. But equally we are excited by the rate of progress in the last two generations. As new avenues of development widen every year, the temptation is to think that it is only a matter of time before we will have all the answers. Clearly, much that was a mystery in the past is already understood, and so it seems that all that is needed is more patience and more money for research to solve the remaining mysteries.

There are certainly still inexplicable phenomena, but the majority in the profession do not think it is necessary to search for their causes anywhere else than in the psychological, physiological and pathological areas we are already so successfully exploring. The well recognized, but not so well understood, interplay of the physical and emotional areas means we can assign a significant number of unexpected or unexplained 'healings' to this area and feel professionally very comfortable. Spontaneous regression is accepted as a satisfactory explanation of other 'healings'.

But I wonder whether these explanations really cover the case of H.P., a missionary friend of mine for many years. Some while ago she was under the care of neuro-surgeons who removed the main bulk of a benign space-occupying lesion which was becoming life-threatening on account of its size. The surgery was highly successful, although the surgeon reported that some portions of lesion could not be removed without unacceptable risk to H.P.'s normal brain tissue. Her friends, who had prayed for the surgeon in his work, were delighted and proceeded to ask God to complete what the surgeon could not. There was, however, eventually a return of symptoms and H.P. returned to the surgeon. After a full reinvestigation, he was convinced that there was a need for further surgery. The friends continued to pray urgently that the tumour might be 'shrunk'. In due course H.P. was allocated a bed and prepared for the reopening of her skull. The surgeon wisely insisted on updating the data that would be available to him in the theatre. After a careful examination of the X-ray scan, he came to her bedside and announced that there was no need for surgery. There was no longer any sign of the tumour. 'An answer to prayer. It's a miracle,' said H.P.

'No,' said the surgeon. 'I must have made a mistake in analysing the data.'

What alternative explanations are available, apart from a diagnostic error? This might be an example of a rarely occurring *spontaneous* regression of a tumour, or it might be a disappearance that happened *specifically* as an answer to prayer. In both cases, a Christian would of course find God involved as Creator, though in rather different ways. With a mind-set induced by tradition and encouraged by research, it is inevitable that a secular, deterministic profession will easily exclude the spiritual altogether.

Facing the Unknown:
A Theologian's View

So far in this chapter, we have been led by a Christian doctor to recognize a *sense of the unknown* which every doctor faces when trying to understand how healing happens. As Dr Lees shows, while medicine tends to be shy about admitting this openly, it often does so implicitly by taking an 'empirical approach', making use of regimes and drugs which appear to be effective, even when there is no complete physiological description of *why* they work.

However, it is notable that Dr Lees does not want to *isolate* God in the area of the unknown, as if we were only talking about a 'God of the gaps'. Such a God would be gradually pushed out of the world as we found increasingly accurate explanations for what at first seems mysterious. Rather, Dr Lees affirms, 'all healing is God's healing', whether we understand the process or not, and whether or not the practitioner is a religious believer. God is at work in promoting healing in areas of the known *and* the unknown. But, if this is so, we shall need to ask why in Christian testimony it has often seemed that the unexpected or the inexplicable healing has been thought to be of special significance, giving special clues to the nature and purpose of God. The answer may not simply be a religious appetite for the sensational.

If we analyse Dr Lees' account more closely, we can detect at least three different kinds of 'unknown' in his experience of how people are healed. First there is *the unknown in the known*. Dr Lees notices a dimension of the mysterious even where medicine has come to a considerable scientific understanding of disease and its cure. Even here, the good therapist will recognize that 'in the final analysis the most we can do is to help or encourage the healing process'.

Second, there is *the not as yet known*, where medical experts hope to understand more fully in due time. Here we can already sketch in advance the kinds of area in which scientific knowledge may arise, and Dr Lees in his account draws attention to at least three. There is the phenomenon of spontaneous remission (of, for example, tumours) whose biology and chemistry we may be able in time to comprehend; there is the interaction between mind and body in a holistic approach to health and medicine; and there are the problems of diagnosis, involving all the human factors of the one who is involved in this operation.

But third, many Christian doctors such as Dr Lees identify instances of healing which appear more baffling, which do not seem amenable to investigation and analysis – at least with any scientific instruments that we have at present or in the conceivable future – and whose explanation they are inclined to say is *unknowable* in scientific terms. That is, they cannot identify the parameters of knowledge within which these events *might* be explained in any future development of the scientific approach. Things thus happen in healing that seem to them to belong in a special way to the mystery of God and his action in the world.

The practice of prayer and the belief that a 'miracle' has occurred seem to have an obvious relevance to this third kind of unknown, though Christian doctors would, I am sure, immediately acknowledge their relevance to events that display the other two sorts of 'unknown' as well. Prayer and miracle are just as appropriate to instances of healing in which a great deal is known about what is happening, and I want to explore this claim a little more below.

However, Dr Lees suggests that the secular 'mind-set', of many doctors prevents their recognizing in particular the third kind of unknown, though he has sometimes found himself confronted by it. As a theologian, I believe that we need to work more closely at defining what this last area of the unknown might be, and to clarify its difference from the first two.

Grace and Nature

The first two 'unknowns' on the one hand, and the third on the other, must surely not be dumped into two separate compartments labelled respectively 'natural' and 'supernatural', or even 'medical' and 'spiritual'. Such a division was possible when God as Creator was conceived as standing back from the world of nature, letting it run as a self-contained entity and perhaps stepping in ('intervening') from time to time to supplant nature and work a miracle instead. This kind of world picture belonged with the view of the universe as an intricate machine, which a Designer could invent, construct and then leave to operate on its own; occasionally he could break in to tinker with the mechanism. So nature could be replaced for a moment with 'supernature', before returning to its accustomed way of behaving.

But modern science has in fact made it impossible for us to think of the world as such a finely-tuned piece of machinery. The biological and the sociological sciences have taught us to understand the world as a community, as an organic whole whose parts interrelate more like a family than a factory. While we may like to think that this is a new insight of our post-Darwinian civilization, it is in fact the picture presented by the Scriptures of the Old and New Testament, where God relates himself to all his creatures in the world. He enters into special covenant relationship with human beings, but he also makes covenant with *all* living creatures (Genesis 9.9–17) receives praise from the music of the trees and the waves (Psalm 96.11–12), plays with the sea-monster in the depths of the ocean (Psalm 104.26) and will respond to the groaning of the universe as he sets it free from decay (Romans 8.18–24). Above all, he has committed himself to the material world by becoming flesh in his Son, Jesus Christ; he immerses himself in the network of relationships within the world and bears the pain of their brokenness in the cross.

Christian believers thus cannot draw on either the ancient Scriptures or modern biology to countenance a division between the natural and supernatural, as if one kind of healing could belong to the first sphere of reality and another to the second. If God involves himself in the community of his world as a covenant partner, then the natural and 'super-natural' (or 'more-than-nature') are always woven together, one never being present without the other. It is better perhaps to talk of 'nature and grace'; God is graciously present and active in his creation, always completing nature by grace. On the one hand there is never nature without grace, as God is never absent from his created community; on the other hand, there is never grace (the transforming presence of God) without a natural basis, that is a place in nature where God comes and which he uses as a place of encounter.

The different kinds of 'unknown' with which we are faced in healing thus point not to events in which God is either absent (less unknown factors) or intervening (more unknown factors), but to different *forms* of his relationship to his creation, different ways in which nature and grace are combined.

When we observe continuous or regular patterns in healing, results which are fairly predictable given the diagnosis and the regimes of treatment applied, we may recognize the continuous creative work of God within nature. Here the elements of the unknown (the *first* and *second* level we have discerned) may be due to such factors as the complex relationship between mind and body, so that though the pattern of recovery is in fact regular we may find it difficult to perceive. At the same time, the sense of unknown areas within the coming of health will serve to make us humble in recognizing the need for grace. It is this kind of humility which the Wisdom writers of the Old Testament commend. As part of their scribal skills they were trained to recognize patterns of cause and effect in the world around, to classify experience and to be able to predict that if x were done, then y would follow; they developed many of the empirical skills that we now find in modern science. But at the same time they admit that there is always an element of the unknown, something unforeseen that can trip up the confident, and through which they could learn 'the fear of the Lord' (Proverbs 16.1–9, for example).

On the other hand the believer will be open to the possibility of God's doing *something new* within nature, something discontinuous with past experience, or exceptional in comparison with the normal pattern of events. This will give rise to the *third* sense of the unknown, for there are no parameters of knowledge within which it can be located. For the reasons I have given above, however, we can speak of a novel event like this as still being *within* nature, and not as a cancelling of nature. It would only be incoherent to think of such a new and unprecedented event as being within nature if we supposed that nature runs, like a machine, by rigid laws in a totally closed system of cause and effect. But, in fact, what we call 'laws of nature' are simply observations of regularity.

At the same time, then, a unique healing will be recognizable as having a *basis* in nature, rooted in some natural area which God has taken hold of and used for something quite new. Though it is perhaps invidious to mention examples, I would myself judge that disappearance of tumours and accelerated knitting of fractures could well fall into this category of events in nature which God has completed in a new way through his grace. By contrast, it is difficult to see any natural basis in claims about total replacement of missing limbs, and I am not surprised that convincing evidence is lacking for this kind of happening. It may well be that the case of H.P. which Dr Lees relates *does* belong to the kind of novel event I have been discussing, where something totally new happens within nature through God's grace. He obviously inclines to think this; without firsthand experience it is hard for the reader to make a judgement, and the alternative explanation remains for a Christian believer, that a spontaneous regression is the result of God's general sustaining grace in the whole universe and so presents us with the first two kinds of 'unknown'.

Cooperation in Healing

With this theological background, we can now attempt a general answer to the question, 'How are people healed?'. There is actually a wider question in the background, which is 'How does God act in the world at all?'. I want now to propose, and to develop my conviction that it is always through a *cooperation* between God and his creation, through divine initiative and creaturely response. God, that is to say, never fulfils his purposes unilaterally. He often takes the initiative in his actions, but the character of his activity is persuasion rather than coercion, influence rather than compulsion, a drawing out of response rather than forcing obedience. This is the divine character which is revealed through the cross of Jesus: 'divine weakness is stronger than human strength'. In his humility God desires the creatures he has made to contribute to his project in creation, to his aim to form truly personal beings. When we speak of 'grace through nature' we should then have in mind a real *partnership* between grace and nature, and the healing process shows this especially clearly.

According to God's purpose, some of this cooperation will take the form of regular patterns of healing and recovery. There is, however, the possibility of the exceptional event, outside the normal patterns. This is not because God overrides nature, or intervenes to break up any usual 'laws' of nature. Rather, we may say that God achieves a level of cooperation with his creation which makes the new and unique happen. While this cannot be entirely explained in terms of the complex interaction between mind and body, our psychosomatic wholeness does seem to provide an opportunity and a space for this kind of cooperation to take place. Our responsiveness to God's desire to heal, whether at a conscious or unconscious level, will be bound to have some effect upon our physical state of being.

But what kind of response are we talking about? There is obviously a danger here of putting all the emphasis upon the faith of the individual person who needs to be healed, with the result of fostering a guilt-complex which will certainly stand in the way of health and wholeness. We have heard the insensitive and damaging accusations that 'You didn't have enough faith' or 'You didn't pray hard enough.' We must catch a much wider vision here of the response that God seeks in his work of healing. In the first place, the work of doctors and medical scientists in developing drugs and applying practical therapy is all part of the responsiveness of his creation which God wants to use. Then there is certainly the conscious attitude of the patient towards recovery, including trust in God and an acceptance and offering of forgiveness; but there is also the response of the body and mind at the subconscious levels to the Spirit of God who searches and knows us even when we were 'knit together in [our] mother's womb' (Psalm 139.13). As I have already hinted, the psychosomatic wholeness of the human being, mysterious though it is, may offer some clue towards the way that response to God might be possible 'in [our] inward parts' (Psalm 139.13).

Moreover, we must look beyond the individual to the place of the whole community; there is the response of the group which surrounds the patient in loving care, and makes common cause with him or her in prayers of faith. This is a constant feature of the stories of healing which Dr Lees records. So, though it is a vast and contentious subject, we cannot avoid some consideration here of the way that prayers of the Christian community assist healing. Such prayer, I am suggesting, is a working together in partnership with God in his desire to heal. In his humility he opens himself to this help from the side of his own world; he chooses to need our intercessions. Only this can make intercessory prayer real and no mere charade or puppet play. It is impossible to rationalize the way in which prayer for others actually affects the situation, but we might follow through a little the insights I have developed above about the world as a community, or a network of interrelationships.

When we pray for the healing of another, we are surely not asking God for something which he could achieve perfectly well unilaterally, but refuses to do until he hears our prayers. Such an understanding of prayer not only raises questions about the moral nature of God, but seems very unjust to the person in need and pain. Rather, as we pray for another person we are expressing our love and concern for her, and God takes that love into his own. He wants to create a response within her at every level (conscious and unconscious) that will promote healing and which will cooperate with his own initiatives of grace. Our love for her and our desire for her health augment and amplify the urgings of his own Spirit, so that together God and the interceders begin to work transformation.

This is, of course, only one insight into the meaning of intercessory prayer, but I offer it as relevant to our question about how people are healed. Healing comes through partnership between God and his creation, and prayer is a means of entering such a partnership. We may ask, however, if the point is the transforming effect of our love, hopes and expectations for someone, why our intercessions should take the form of a *request* to God. Actually, I notice that they often may not, as language like 'simply lifting her before God' or 'placing her in God's hands' is increasingly being used in prayer. But for all that, it is quite proper for our loving concern for another to take the form of asking God for something; we are expressing what we would fervently wish to happen within the context of a child-parent relationship where requests are natural.

Blockages to Healing

People are healed by the action of God's grace through nature, in cooperation with his creatures. This is the proposal I have been making as a theologian, arising from reflection upon a Christian doctor's testimony. Why, then, are people *not* healed? No theological account can avoid this question, just as no theology should presume to know the whole answer to it.

One traditional answer is that God has a purpose in permitting suffering. I use the language of 'permission' quite deliberately, as I do not find the belief that God directly *causes* suffering to be in accord with the biblical picture of a God who grieves and suffers in sympathy with his people. To say that God suffers with us means that he takes upon himself the vulnerability and weakness of love, and is on the side of the victims not the torturers.[1] God gives his creation freedom, and suffering emerges when it drifts away from his purpose; he permits this, and freely suffers the consequences with us.

But we need to think carefully about this traditional answer in the light of *partnership* in healing between God and human persons. For God to 'permit' suffering cannot mean that he refrains from taking an action that would *inevitably* result in healing, regardless of response. Rather it must mean that he refrains from initiating actions of grace that *could* produce physical healing *if they were* met by the appropriate response from the human side. One context in which this permissive will of God is exercised is the normal process of ageing. According to the biblical view of the world, death at the right time, 'full of years', is the proper end to life that God intends. His purpose is not for endless and prolonged life in this particular body, but for eternal life and resurrection. However, we must immediately add that death as we actually know it is an ambiguous power; it is 'a good thing spoilt'. It has been warped and distorted by sin, by the sliding of the whole natural world away from the purpose of God. It retains the remnant of goodness that God intended for it, but it is also now hostile and destructive, breaking relationships of love by coming in an untimely way. Thus

19

the apostle Paul can call death 'the last enemy'. Death *as it is* is not what God meant it to be, and so we can envisage situations where God will initiate actions to prevent its befalling us, and when it will be right for us in cooperation with God to resist its onslaught.

Taking up the theme of God's permissive will, we may say, nevertheless, that it is *possible* that God's aim for our life may include permitting even untimely death, or a crippling disease or handicap. It is *possible* that he wants to use this situation for his own loving purposes, to bring out of it some growth and virtue in the life of the sufferer or those who care for him. However, we need to be very cautious about making such a judgement. The declared intention of God, as we discern it in the Scriptures, is to bring about wholeness of life; this means that we need to have very good reason indeed to think otherwise than that God desires us to know health in every way. The balance of doubt must always be on the side of God's desire for our healing, though of course he can still redeem situations where healing is not achieved, and bring good out of a suffering that he neither planned nor wants to continue.

In other words, we must say that the main reason people are not healed is because God is frustrated in his aim to bring health and wholeness. He experiences the pain of failing, at least in the short term, to bring peace (*shalom*) into human life, as the prophets of the Old Testament make abundantly clear. They constantly portray a God who is disappointed that the covenant has been broken from the human side, who sets out with great expectations for his people and finds these to be frustrated, and who feels anguish for his people as disaster overtakes them. Christian disciples are thus called to follow in the way of the cross, in the sense that they are called to 'serve the pain of God'[2] and to 'stand by God in the hour of his grief '.[3]

This kind of understanding belongs with the whole perspective of a God who works in partnership, who has chosen in the very act of creation to be at least partly dependent upon his creatures in bringing about his purposes.[4] In this partnership God retains his sovereignty, first because he does not have the method of cooperation forced upon him from outside; he freely chooses it in his desire to make persons. Second, he shows his sovereign power in never finally being defeated when his human partners fail to work with him and break their covenant with him;

he is always free to take new initiatives, to open up the relationship again and to draw out response. *People therefore are healed through a process of cooperation between God and his world, and when they are not healed cooperation has broken down.*

But here we must take a very wide view indeed about the scope of this 'cooperation'. We must be especially careful not to throw the burden of blame for its breaking down simply – or indeed at all – upon the *particular* participants in any situation where healing is needed, and who are called to be open in trust to God. To put the weight on their response would certainly produce a whole heap of false guilt. The resistance to cooperation that God meets in his world is a very complex story, and one that we can usually hardly comprehend at all. Of course, God *can* be frustrated in his work by a lack of response which *could* have been offered in the immediate situation, either by the individual sufferer or by the community of carers around him or her. But this is only one small thread in a whole tapestry of relationship between God and his world.

There are many forces and influences outside the immediate situation which present lack of response to God. There is a whole network of factors in which the sufferer is caught, including genetic and social elements. We are each bound up with the whole of humanity ('in Adam', as the apostle Paul puts it), and we inherit the consequences of others' actions in the past which shape the nature of human beings in physiological, mental and spiritual ways. To give a concrete example, it seems that the slipping of the world away from God's purpose over millennia of years has resulted in a situation in which there are (at the present moment) obstacles to God's desire to heal those who suffer from the AIDS virus in its developed form. Wherever healing does not come, whether it is mental or physical, there are hidden factors in the fallen world which for the moment the combined influence of God's love, the prayers of loving people and the gifts of medical science cannot overcome. At the same time we must not lose hope in God's promise to make a new creation in which 'neither shall there be mourning nor crying nor pain any more, for the former things have passed away' (Revelation 21.4 RSV).

When healing does not happen despite prayers of faith, and decline in health does not seem to be due to a normal ageing process, we may therefore expect there to be a whole complex of hidden factors that are preventing God's aim for wholeness being fulfilled. We must not be overconfident about our ability to unravel them, or reduce the complications to a simplicity that feeds our ego and sense of power over others more than it reflects reality. We may add that lack of proper response to God's desire for our health may in fact result in a 'cure' in which certain symptoms disappear, but which is not true 'healing' in the sense of the restoring of the whole person to health in mind, body and spirit. On the other hand, God can still bring about a 'healing' in the sense of spiritual wholeness where various factors prevent the curing of physical ailments.

The Reality of the Demonic: A Doctor's View

Coming back into the discussion at this point, I must say that I find the emphasis of Dr Fiddes upon cooperation in healing to be most helpful, and an approach with which I greatly empathize. As a background to the specific partnership in healing, it is a wonder in itself that the Creator should involve humankind in the management of the environment when he clearly did not need such help (see Genesis 1.26). However, beside any lack of cooperation from us we must add at this point that there is another factor which can block healing, and which needs to be dealt with in any discussion of the spiritual dimension within healing. I mean the reality of the demonic.

The secular, deterministic mind-set among doctors that I referred to earlier will, of course, exclude the demonic along with miracles. To introduce the biblical affirmation of some relationship between health and demons is likely to be seen as a return to medieval patterns of understanding as well as being totally unnecessary. For Christian doctors, however, the New Testament witness to the reality of demons cannot be escaped.

In my view, a good deal of confusion in this area is caused by excessive claims. Today we find Christians talking of 'the spirit of anger or lust' or some other 'spirit' as dominating a person's life, and then praying for deliverance. I suspect that Satan is delighted at having encouraged people to see the 'works of the flesh' as always being manifestations of particular demons. So instead of accepting that they have a problem with 'the flesh' (that is, the whole human being in its orientation against God), they attribute the problem directly to the enemy. Instead of cooperating with *the* Spirit in 'mortifying the flesh' they seek 'deliverance' from 'a spirit' and ignore the problem of the flesh as a general and ongoing area that needs the continual attention of a man or woman in Christ.

However, excessive claims or an unbiblical view of demonic activity should not be allowed to blind us to the existence of evil spirits. The ultimate triumph for the enemy of humankind is so to obscure the fact of his existence that he can work unnoticed and not be discussed. In this context, let me share a learning experience within my own family. We were missionaries at the time and had been in Asia for twelve years. We had the privilege of seeing a number of churches established. My wife, Shirley, had always had a vivid imagination but due to an increasing political instability in the area, the prospect of dreadful political disasters began to grow greater and greater in her thinking. There came a point when her anxiety was so acute that she refused to read any newspapers or listen to the news broadcasts. As a Christian husband and as a medical person, I of course sought to support her in every possible way. It was like fighting a rearguard action and failing to hold back a flood. Eventually something we picked up from the Christian author Corrie ten Boom alerted us to a possible cause of the problem that had not even crossed our minds.

On reflection we were aware that in Shirley's home, theosophy and some associated spiritual healing had a place and Shirley had been slightly involved. Since the time of her conversion to Christ she had thought no more about any spiritist involvement. Ten Boom's illustration opened our eyes to new ideas. 'Imagine', she writes, 'a patrol being sent out into no-man's land during a lull in the fighting, to explore the enemies' defences. The patrol leader drops his compass into deep mud and it is lost. The group attempt to navigate by the stars but that helps little on an overcast night. Inadvertently they move into enemy territory and are captured'.[5] Her point is that a deliberate or accidental excursion into enemy territory potentially exposes us to being 'captured'.

In our ignorance and desperation we entered into cooperation with God; we prayed that if Shirley's problems related to some access that 'the enemy' had in her childhood, she should receive deliverance from this influence in the name of the Christ who had received 'all authority in heaven and earth' and who at the cross became the victor over Satan. It was as if a wet suffocating blanket of pathological fear were immediately lifted. Only once more did Shirley find herself being overwhelmed and that was when she was alone in a remote situation when rumours were rife during a period of particular political instability. She prayed for the specific protection of the victory of Christ and the wet blanket lifted. After that she was able to live with whatever happened without a crushing and paralysing fear overtaking her.

Healing in an Animistic Context: The Experience of a Missionary Doctor

This experience leads me on to reflect that praying for the sick in an animistic situation, where all sickness is perceived as spiritual in origin and only the spirits are seen as a source of healing, is very different from our position in the secular western world. People of animistic background realize there must be a god (who created the sun, moon, mountains, rivers and so on) but assume there is no point in paying attention to him because he has never done anyone any harm. The spirits, however, are to be feared as sources of harm and so are to be placated. In my career as a missionary doctor I found it necessary to teach that Jesus is stronger than Satan, that he came to destroy the works of Satan (see 1 John 3.8) and to open a way of forgiveness.

In the context of such a message I was inevitably asked to pray for the sick. This came as a shock to a young missionary doctor, especially when he felt particularly vulnerable, had no diagnostic aids, virtually no medicines, and was miles from anywhere. I explained that God had helped people to discover some medicines which I could use. But whether or not I had suitable medication I had to pray, for the honour of Jesus was at stake. I explained that he does not heal everyone, but still I had to pray. I was then surprised by some unexpected outcomes.

At first I was reluctant to participate in this praying, lacking an understanding of the spiritual situation. I saw a priority in seeking to teach that beside spiritual forces, there were natural forces, such as bacteria. But as time went on it seemed to me that God's gracious purpose was that the power of Christ over Satan had to be demonstrated to the Tagal people. I believe that God saved my life without my realizing it, and that he did so in a mysterious way that resulted in a message being heralded up and down the valley that the spirit protecting me was stronger than any spirits known in the valley at the time. Many people turned to Christ for life and salvation in a way that I found hard to explain at the time. Twenty-eight years later, in the company of 1,500 local Christians, I was astonished to hear for the first time a story about my deliverance from death; it was reported that a man had tried to kill me, but had been unable to withdraw his jungle knife from his scabbard. This had been clearly seen as a direct act of the God I proclaimed.

Healing and the Power of Evil: A Theological Response

When we are thinking about the complex mass of factors that can thwart the desire of God to achieve healing, we do need to listen to the experience of Christian people through the ages about the power of evil. They speak of cosmic spiritual forces which can, in certain circumstances, hinder healing. While God's ultimate victory over evil is certain, and the battle against radical evil has been won in principle in the cross of Jesus, evil still has a hold upon human minds and hearts such that God cannot always draw out the response that he desires.

We must not miss the fact that when the New Testament writers refer to 'the principalities and powers' they have partly in mind the *structural* forms that sin takes in our world. There are oppressive bureaucracies, totalitarian states, and forces of national-ism and ideology that restrict freedom and spoil life. Even the best structures of authority can 'become demonic', more concerned with maintaining themselves in being than serving people, and demanding a loyalty that should belong only to God. Sin is a social power. But when the apostle Paul uses the phrase 'principalities and powers' he is *also* thinking of cosmic forces in the spiritual realm that have become distorted and destructive. Bearing in mind this dual meaning there can, therefore, be an unholy alliance between individual human sinfulness and 'the powers' of *every* kind; the result is to block human response to God.

So God desires to bring healing, but his creation fails to cooperate. What other explanation can we give, for example, for the unspeakable horrors of Auschwitz? While God ultimately permitted the freedom in his universe that was misused and so brought forth this mountain of evil, I find it totally impossible to suppose that he permitted Auschwitz in the *direct* sense of being able to step in and stop it unilaterally and choosing not to do so. Surely we must say that God fervently desired to turn the hearts of the oppressors to himself in repentance and to bring health in that place of hellish destruction, but that he was frustrated in his aims by the 'principalities and powers' of organized evil at every level – in the human heart, in the power structures of the state and in the spiritual realm.

It is possible that hostile cosmic forces are also involved in resistance to God's desire to heal in less dramatic situations. Dr Lees chooses to place a fair amount of emphasis upon this in his account, though he also offers some wise cautions against excessive interest in 'demonic activity'. It is important to make clear that Christian people will differ in the way that they conceive of these 'powers of darkness'. Some – like Dr Lees in his account – will envisage them as having personality, and will recognize the figure of 'the Satan' as a disembodied person of ultimate evil. Others will judge that while radical evil can only be talked about by personifying (using personal language when talking about it), it actually lacks any real 'personality' of its own. They think this because the effect of evil is always to depersonalize, while it is the mark of a person always to be able to make others more personal. Since evil powers cannot enhance the personality of others, it may be argued (and I would myself take this view) that the personality they seem to exhibit comes from being parasitic upon human persons.

But such differences in understanding surely need not undermine agreement about some common elements of experience – that there is an objective power and reality of evil, a dark reservoir of hostility to God's purposes, which is larger than any individual's sins and into which the individual can stray. Dr Lees here aptly quotes an image from Corrie ten Boom about 'moving inadvertently into enemy territory'. While the experience of Christians from earliest times has been that when radical evil is manifested in a personified form it is overcome by being confronted directly with a declaration of the Lordship of Christ, there are many situations when the powers of darkness are not exposed in the open like this, and their influence is more subtle and harder to deal with. They are part of the hidden factors that lie behind a thwarting of God's desire for wholeness, and their hiddenness should help to prompt our caution about any claim to know what has caused the blockage in healing.

A Doctor's Conclusion: Humility About the Unknown

An understanding of healing today is sadly hampered by the positions our training and experience cause us to establish and then defend. While doctors recognize areas of the unknown in healing, they have a problem in admitting too freely to ignorance as that does not help 'patient confidence' which they want to maintain. Those deeply involved in Christian healing have a problem too. When healings and deliverance have occurred it is probably difficult to avoid exaggeration. Those who pray for sufferers, and particularly those who believe they have a special gift of healing will be encouraging each other to look for the results of faith. Any objective or critical analytical response would appear to verge on a lack of faith. So the tendency to overclaim is built into the situation as strongly as the medical world is predisposed in the opposite direction. The result is a defence of positions rather than either side being fully open to the reality of the situation.

Those who place a large emphasis on the reality of healings frequently quote the words of Jesus to support their belief that we should be much more expectant of miracles. But I cannot see why the Lord's promise to his disciples who have faith that they 'will do even greater things than these, because I am going to the Father' (John 14.12 NIV), should apply primarily to healing. Jesus' acts of healing included a paralytic, presumably with contraction of the muscles, who is reported to have walked immediately. At a physical level, could anyone do greater things than the healings attributed to Jesus? Some of the 'greater things' I have rejoiced to see have been the human heart which is 'deceitful above all things and beyond cure', touched by his patient love and turned voluntarily to Christ and his cross for forgiveness and new birth. To see a whole community transformed, and the magistrates put out of business for three years looks like a work of the Spirit (started through two young boys) that has no parallel in the Gospels. Would that not be a 'greater work', although no-one in the area of the Kelabit highlands of East Malaysia where this happened, claimed it as such? By contrast, there are many situations in which signs and wonders have had very limited impact. Pharaoh had a significant exposure to wonders but his late positive response was short-lived. Jesus said, 'they will not be convinced even if someone rises from the dead' (Luke 16.31 NIV).

This does not mean God does not heal in answer to prayer and sometimes uses healing to touch the hearts of people. However, our tendency to set up God's healing as proof of his power is commonly associated with some greater or lesser degree of overstatement. This has to be an invitation for an opposite reaction from secularists who look in from outside on what is going on. A readiness to admit that we might be wrong in some aspects of our understanding of the data, or that in listening we may to some degree have missed the point, will lead to more progress in the meeting of minds between doctors and those involved in spiritual healing. What is certain is that it is the same God who prospers both unbelieving and believing doctors in their work with patients and in their research towards health.

A Theologian's Conclusion: Wonder About the Unknown

In reflecting upon Dr Lees' opening statement, I began by noting the areas of the unknown which a Christian doctor is willing to recognize. All three areas of the unknown, we must affirm, can be occasions for grace, that is for the coming of wholeness and the transforming of personality. Furthermore, there will come moments in *all three areas* when grace seems to be 'focused' in a special way and a sense of wonder is aroused in us. A 'miracle' is an event which creates 'wonder', that shakes us out of our everyday perception of the world so that we find we are being grasped by a reality which is ultimate and lays a claim upon us. An event – in this case of healing – suddenly becomes transparent to the presence and power of God; it 'takes on depth', and we 'notice dimensions in the event that normally escape us'.[6] God's grace is present in all healing, whether it seems ordinary or remarkable, but the event may not always take on this quality of disclosure for us, and arouse this sense of wonder. When it does, we feel that a 'miracle' has happened.

Thus, a recovery even within the ordinary patterns of healing can suddenly take on the depth of miracle. It does not *have* to be an extraordinary event in itself. Nevertheless, such a view of miracle does not at all exclude the third kind of 'unknown' I have described above, the event which seems to stand outside all regularities and expected outcomes. To find miracle within what is continuous and repeatable in nature does not rule out its happening as an event which has no precedent. When God gains such cooperation from his creation that something really new can take place within nature, for which science has no existing model of explanation ready, then the unknown leads us to wonder.

Moreover, the boundaries between the three kinds of 'unknown' (the unknown in the known, the not as yet known, and the unknowable) are not as sharp as I have made them appear for the sake of classification. At any time we may find that what we thought we *could* know has nevertheless led us into the mystery of God. Likewise, when we hope in God's new creation we find that mysteries of healing only seem 'unknowable' because we are using the scientific tools that necessarily belong to the old creation in which we live at present. One day 'we shall know as we are known', and then we shall no longer see through a glass darkly, but face to face (1 Corinthians 13.12 AV).

References

1. Biblical texts that seem to present God as directly making people suffer must, I suggest, be understood in a variety of ways depending upon context. They all reflect the Hebrew idiom of simply stating the final cause (God is the only Creator of the world and the only Lord of history) and leaving out the intermediate causes (e.g. the evils of a fallen world). Within this idiom, some texts present God as causing suffering directly as judgement, when careful reading discovers that God's judgement takes the form of 'letting his people go' their own way and reaping the inherent consequences of their own sins (e.g. Hosea 11.5–9). Some texts

present the truth that we suffer as the victims of other people's actions (Jeremiah 31.29). Other texts see suffering as a form of discipline, where we may understand that the possibility of suffering provides educational guidelines about growth and development (if you touch fire you will get burnt).

2. K. Kitamori, *Theology of the Pain of God*, tr. M.E. Bratcher (SCM 1966), pp. 50, 53ff.

3. D. Bonhoeffer, *Letters and Papers from Prison*, the enlarged edition, tr. R. Fuller and J. Bowden (SCM 1971), p. 347.

4. For a further exposition of this, see P.S. Fiddes, *The Creative Suffering of God* (Oxford University Press 1988), pp. 63–76.

5. C. ten Boom, *Defeated Enemies* (Christian Literature Crusade 1973), p. 10.

6. For this phrase, see J. Macquarrie, *Principles of Christian Theology*, revised edition (SCM 1977), p. 252.

CHAPTER 2

The Church's Ministry of
Healing Today

Bishop Graham Dow
Dr Trevor Stammers

*Dr Bill Lees has written about his personal experience of a healing
ministry as a missionary doctor. This chapter surveys what is
happening in the context of local churches. Because it arises from the
experience of its authors, a doctor involved in a local general medical
practice and a non-conformist church in London and a Church of
England minister who developed a healing ministry in a parish church
in Coventry, it inevitably draws largely on what is happening in
England (though Graham Dow has also had some experience of
healing ministry in Pakistan). However, it raises general questions of
principle and practice which are applicable in very different situations.
In the appendix, Bishop Dow provides tried and tested ways of
training church members for healing ministry and suggests formats for
various types of healing services.*

The Ministry of Healing
as Practised by Christians

Nature and Grace:
The Natural and the Spiritual

Nature cannot be separated from God, as other chapters make clear.
Biblical faith indicates that God is active and present in all nature;
what is more he does things which are not fully understood and
which cause people to wonder. The lines between the so-called
natural and supernatural are never clear; nor should they be, for

God the Creator is in everything. He does not stand back, as it were, so that some things happen just by nature, even nature which he has created. The order and regularity of the universe is a great gift to us, but we cannot therefore say that God is not always actively present and perhaps doing by his Spirit what is not fully understood or perceived to be regular.

We must, therefore, affirm a unity between approaches to healing which might be called 'natural' and those which might be called 'spiritual'. All is God's gift to humankind. The so-called 'natural' belongs to the created world over which human beings are to exercise 'creative management' (see Genesis 1.26–28). We are to develop the world, under God, for the good of all. The creation, we are told is good, and human beings, as those created in God's image, are presumably expected to exercise creativity in their stewardship of God's world.

The so-called 'spiritual', in which grace is received through prayer is also God's gift to us. Within the realm of nature God hears our requests and things change for the better without us knowing exactly how. The spiritual and the natural are fully integrated in humanity as God intended it to be. We do well, therefore, to make good use of the secrets of God's creation as we have discovered them and good use of the fellowship of prayer, the personal intimacy with God into which, through Christ, we are privileged to enter. God has called us into partnership with him, partnership in the spiritual and partnership in the natural, in which he is also fully present and active.

The Christian need have no fear of making the fullest use of the natural means of healing. All that is discovered in the natural and behavioural sciences is God's truth. We are foolish if we try to boil an electric kettle by praying over it. We plug it in. Similarly, all that God has given in the healing sciences is to be received and put to good use. People, of course, are much more complex than electric kettles; truly we are wonderfully made. In humility, therefore, and in recognition of our creatureliness before our Creator and Healer we do well also to pray about our healing. There is no reason why we should not pray as we plug in the kettle, perhaps in thanksgiving for God's gifts. But a sense of proportion is necessary. The degree of human mastery differs from the kettle to the body, and human beings, unlike kettles, are created in the image of God. There continues to be a large dimension of the unknown about how human beings 'tick', and expression of our dependence upon God is appropriate.

Biblical faith teaches us that prayer is central, not peripheral to our existence. It is the expression of the partnership with God into which we have been called. We have been created to please God, to glorify him. In this we are totally dependent on him in a day by day sense. Apart from his loving will we cannot exist. Therefore in whatever way Christian believers sense the need for healing of body, mind or relationships, they will make that a matter of prayer to God. Similarly, in expression of concern for another's health, there will be prayer to God as well as practical advice about avenues of professional help.

There is nothing odd about focusing concern for one another in active prayer, when in company together and where hands may be laid on as a sign of healing in response to prayer. Western society operates in a very privatized way where we prefer to emphasize silent private prayer. The New Testament challenges us equally to see our place in a family of God, a fellowship of belonging in which the things of Christ are constantly shared. Paul writes of his need of prayers (see, for example, Romans 15.30–32; Colossians 4.3). That centrality of prayer for one another will take in our healing needs and can be given tangible focus appropriately in our Christian fellowships.

The Christian Professional

The Christian doctor, surgeon, counsellor, psychiatrist or social worker is aware of the spiritual and natural dimensions of the wholeness they work for. They will commit their work to God in prayer. For them to pray for their clients as they actually use their skills is most appropriate. Grace and nature will be in full operation together and in harmony. On occasion it may be possible to pray aloud with the client, when there is agreement concerning the place of spiritual values. There is, then, a united sense of dependence upon God, to whom we owe our existence day by day, and upon whom our wholeness totally depends.

So Christian professionals will both pray and use their professional skill to the full. As it is for the doctor, so it will also be for the Christian lawyer or Christian educationalist. It will be the same for the Christian minister in the pastoral ministry of the Church and for the Christian worker in any occupation concerned with human well-being. But why not, also, the Christian engineer or research chemist? All human daily occupations only have value in as much as they contribute to human well-being and fulfil God's instructions to develop the world.

In Search of Wholeness

No one is fully whole, nor will be until the Kingdom of God is complete. Our bodies 'groan in travail' until that time and we are less than complete in our emotions, attitudes and relationships. Yet, as other chapters have shown, the overwhelming testimony of the Scriptures is that God wants our healing and is working for this.

Faced with their own needs, sometimes general and quite manageable, and sometimes acute and seriously debilitating, Christians use all that God has given to seek wholeness. Prayer will be made and the doctor consulted.

The fellowship of Christians in the local church need not be asked to share in every small ailment nor in what is personal and inappropriate to share, but equally, to resist the offer of Christians to pray, with remarks like, 'There are many worse off than me', is foolish. There is in western society a pride which makes us think we should manage by ourselves. No, let us welcome gladly the offers of our fellow Christians to pray for us, even then and there.

The whole range of professional services is available to help us and should be used. All truth is God's truth. Nor need Christians suppose that they must consult only a Christian practitioner. The grace with which God upholds the world day by day clearly allows all people to share in the knowledge and blessings of his world, regardless of their faith or lack of it. Good psychiatrists will make use of the rigorous insights of their own discipline. Why should a Christian hesitate to use this expertise? Nevertheless, such is the complexity of human life that questions of values quickly arise. There is not agreement among all professionals, particularly in the human sciences, as to the place of faith and religion, for example, and the status of moral norms which Christians understand to belong to the will of God as revealed by Scripture. Thus a practitioner who is not a Christian might recommend an abortion or a steady sexual relationship outside marriage, when Christians firmly believe these to be contrary to the will of God for them.

Such clashes of values are found increasingly in many disciplines as the Christian heritage of western Europe, sadly, is discarded. They arise, for example, in education, with different understandings of the nature of humanity and its potential, different views about the basis for morality, the place of faith and worship, and the objectivity or otherwise of religious truth. When basic values are agreed between helper and client there is a more realistic possibility of an adult-responsible decision by the client to take the steps offered by the professional helper. There is, therefore, a strong case for consulting a Christian professional in the situations where differences of values are likely to be important.

Doctors readily agree that their work with patients addresses a great deal more than simply providing medical remedies based upon scientific research. People must be addressed as whole beings. The privilege of the doctor's role in western society gives them opportunity for advice at many levels of the client's need. Christians will often find a Christian doctor particularly helpful, and there is the additional blessing of the sense together of prayerful dependence upon God.

'Alternative Medicines'

Western society has recently seen the growth in popularity of a variety of remedial techniques which have not been associated with mainline medicine. Most of these techniques are well-known in other parts of the world, particularly in parts where medicine is less well developed. Among the most sought after are acupuncture, aromatherapy and homeopathy. There is considerable difference among Christians about how to understand and respond to these 'alternatives'. Is the scientific basis of them suspect, or is it that we simply do not yet know sufficient about them to understand this aspect of nature?

The use of natural substances for healing, where there is evidence to support healthy outcome, is clearly positive. Questions, however, need to be asked where treatment is associated with a mysterious, but undefined, 'life force', (homeopathy). According to present scientific understanding, the dilution of homeopathic medicines is so great as to be likely not to include a molecule of the curing substance. What then is happening? When we are told, as Indian practitioners told me, that shaking the potion ten times gives tenfold power, shaking 100 times gives hundredfold power, then it seems that one is in the realm of superstition. Christians should use and practise curative techniques for which a good account can be given, while bearing in mind that there is a great deal about God's world yet to be discovered.

Concerning acupuncture, which is widely practised in the east, it is unclear whether the pressure points at which the needles are placed are natural to the body, with physical effect by the needles, or whether there are other explanations. The authors of this chapter would seriously question the use of techniques, such as homeopathy or acupuncture which invoke an unspecified force to which the cure is attributed.

Wounded Healers

As we think about our own part in giving and receiving healing we recognize that we are all wounded people. Most have been hurt and know pain in our own life history. This does not disqualify us. Rather, here is an authentic basis for sharing in the pain of others. We have a Saviour and Healer whose suffering and death on a cross lies at the heart of our faith. He identified with and bore our sins and our condition. Our healing ministry flows not from our own strength but from our dependence upon God. Our woundedness helps this and makes our message that God heals authentic.

The Ministry of Healing in the Life of the Church

An Integrated Approach

The integrated approach which we have already advocated is what we contend for in the ministry of healing offered by a local church. In some churches the emphasis might be all on professional skills and not on prayer; in other churches, the other way round. A firm emphasis on both is much better.

A growing number of churches have a doctor's practice on the premises as a witness to the unity of spiritual and medical healing. There are Christian medical practices which employ a trained counsellor. A more comprehensive vision has been brought to birth in the St Marylebone Centre, London, where services of prayer with laying on of hands are regularly held. Teams of counsellors are trained both for pastoral and spiritual ministry as well as for more professional counselling. There is a doctors practice and certain other therapies are available.

Most local churches are not going to be host to a medical practice. The integrated approach can be worked out in many simpler ways. Those with pastoral and spiritual responsibility can know where to draw on professional advice and resources when dealing with the needs of those who seek help. In some congregations there are doctors or social workers who can be consulted in confidence and who can be a valuable resource in training people in pastoral skills and insight. Church leaders need to have good links with professional people in the community so that there is exchange of expertise. As we have said, all truth represented in the caring professions is God's truth. To ignore it and to suppose that we can solve most problems by prayer or pastoral counselling is arrogance. Time-consuming though it is to build networks linking pastoral ministers to other professionals in the caring professions, the result will be a more complete ministry.

The Debate About Prayer for Healing

It is hardly surprising that the practice of prayer for healing by the churches generates a great deal of controversy. Any particular form of practice reflects:

(a) A 'world-view', that is, a way in which realities are understood in a particular culture. For example, is the possibility of action by God that is not according to the expected medical or natural patterns (commonly called 'supernatural') allowed or thought likely?

(b) An interpretation of the Bible passages which refer to the healing work of Jesus and the early Christian Church.

(c) An understanding of what we mean by 'healing'.

(d) A view of the causes and purpose of suffering and illness.

Christians do not share a consensus of understanding in these four areas and therefore are often critical of one another's practice and the arguments that support it. Healing touches all of us personally since all of us are ill from time to time and certainly have friends and relatives who face serious illness. We cannot therefore remain detached in the face of the arguments; we adopt our own point of view with its implications for our prayers for healing. We have an investment, personally, in our position. But we also find it difficult to hear those who take a different point of view; we are liable to mishear or misrepresent what is being said or done. It is probably as well to be aware of these factors right from the beginning as we begin to discuss in more detail the practice of prayer and laying on of hands for healing.

On the positive side there is no doubt that prayer for healing is growing in the churches and with a broad measure of support. It is becoming accepted that the Church has a significant part to play in the ministry of healing, and that prayer with the laying on of hands is appropriate for many people at certain times. We believe that God does answer prayer and that healing is one of the ways he responds to our needs. What is more at issue is how the Church should practise prayer for healing, with what expectations and with what understanding of the spiritual realities.

POINTS OF AGREEMENT

In this debate about the practice of healing ministry today and the assumptions that undergird it there are several points of general agreement. It will help to summarize these.

Healing Is a Very Broad Concept

This is argued for in Chapter 3. The goal of Christian healing is that we should be whole people, a goal that is complete as we are whole in company with others, that is in our relationships. Jesus came to bring us 'full life', true freedom. The 'shalom' (peace) promised in the Old Testament is total harmony when all relationships are right including, supremely, that with God.

The Ministry of Healing Includes a Very Wide Range of Practices

The natural and behavioural sciences undergird these practices. We must include those services provided in the community: medicine, public health and health education, psychiatry, counselling, community development and support, drop-in centres. Furthermore, it is increasingly being recognized that concern for the environment is a major factor in promoting health. There is also the simple work of loving and caring, which is not confined to Christians, but which churches should do well. Friendship and visiting help people to feel accepted, and give them a sense of belonging. The way people are made welcome when they come to church is a healing process for many people.

Since our relationship with God is fundamental to human well-being, the spiritual and pastoral ministry of churches, helping people to respond to the word of God, is a vital element in healing. So putting this alongside prayer for healing and all the professional and social ministries mentioned above, we stress the importance of an integrated approach to healing including all the practices available.

Medicine Is Highly Valued as God's Gift

Medicine has developed as a result of the normal process of discovery of the world God has made. To use it to the full is therefore common sense and Christians should not think that God is somehow glorified more if people are healed without it. Medicine is the natural direction in which to look for help in our society as it has developed. It follows that healing by prayer is not 'better' than healing by any other means.

There Are Many Needs Which Medical Science Cannot Meet

This reminds us that all our human sciences are very limited. Nevertheless, prayer is not just to be used when other means fail.

There Is No Clear Division Between the So-called Natural and the Supernatural

No such distinction is drawn in Scripture. Rather, we are invited to affirm God's active involvement with his world at all times. Who knows where the lines are drawn between the natural and the supernatural since everything moves by the energy of God? The word 'miracle' in our present-day sense is unhelpful because it is usually taken to imply that what has happened 'ought' not to happen or cannot happen. In its derivation, however, it means something to be wondered at and this is the sense in which Scripture speaks of the works of Jesus. They are signs of God and his Kingdom but not necessarily contrary to nature.

ASSUMPTIONS IN WESTERN SOCIETY

There is also considerable agreement in the way certain assumptions in western society should be challenged.

Assumption 1 The normal procedure for dealing with sickness is to seek the help of a doctor. The doctor will then refer you to a specialist if treating the condition is beyond his or her level of competence.

We have already affirmed that the discoveries of medical science give a common sense basis for looking to medicine in the case of illness. There is a tendency in the popular consciousness, (but not in the medical profession) for medical science to be thought to be almost omnicompetent in the field of illness. People therefore turn to prayer ministry, if they turn at all, as a last resort. In other cultures such as in Pakistan, where medical resources are considerably more scarce than in the west, people go much more readily for help of a spiritual kind. Muslims go to shrines there; the ministry they receive often has occult features in it. If they think that Christians can do better they will readily ask for healing in Christian meetings or services.

Western society has much to learn from other cultures. Without taking anything from the importance of medicine and other healing sciences we do well to complement the assumption above with an emphasis on the place of prayer as a first resort with a sense of dependence on God. Medicine can then be used prayerfully as well as spiritual resources through healing ministry.

Assumption 2 Supernatural events do not occur, or if they do, only very rarely. God, if he exists, does not change things. The universe operates according to 'laws' which are discovered by empirical science. Healing practice based on scientific discovery is the way to tackle all disorder.

The Bible, on the other hand, offers us another 'world-view'. God is active continually in his creation 'sustaining all things by his powerful word' (Hebrews 1.3). Since the energy of creation is God's energy, there is no problem about his activity that is out of the ordinary, indeed we are never encouraged in Scripture to think that such things ought not to happen.

Assumption 3 Good health is a high priority in my life and is largely attainable through medical science.

It is natural for people to look for good health. To suppose that it is almost their right and is attainable is to be unaware of the complexities of modern life and the importance of spiritual values. There is still too little understanding that patterns of western society are contributing to disease through stress, overwork, loneliness, isolation from community life and the breakdown of intimate relationships. The socialist movements in eastern Europe produced similar results. Easy transport and mobility bring settled community relationships to an end in any society. Rather than face the implications of the kind of society we have developed most people prefer to go on hoping that the medical profession will keep them healthy.

At the same time, there is a growing disillusionment with humanist scientific rationalism which can no longer answer the questions that many people are asking. Alternative medicines, with little scientific basis, are being widely sought after. Interest in Christian healing ministry today reflects the same search. The Christian gospel, however, addresses the issue of sin more than the healing of body or emotions. For that reason we believe that the practice of the ministry of healing must not present health as if it were the foremost goal of our existence, nor must it sidestep rigorous thinking.

The Christian recognizes that the desire for health must be set in the wider context of obedience to the will of God. There are occasions in Scripture when illness or disaster are allowed by God for the sake of another purpose. This does not mean that God does not generally seek to heal. One interpretation should not be pressed to fit all occasions. But to live before God in worship and surrender remains the chief goal.

Assumption 4 Participation in church life is seen either as a religious duty or as a hobby for those who like that sort of thing. Sadly it is not seen as where people can find the blessings of forgiveness of sin or of wholeness of body, mind and spirit that God longs for us to receive.

In the past there were times when it was understood that one went to church to receive forgiveness of sin. A revival of such an awareness is greatly needed. In the lifetime of Jesus, however, people flocked to him to receive healing and hear his teaching. The particular blessings around which any generation may focus will vary but we must pray for church again to be seen as the place where the blessings of God are available.

It would take a whole book to write about all the avenues of Christian healing and most of what is mentioned above is not controversial. In concentrating in the rest of the chapter on the ministry of prayer with laying on of hands we do not want it to be thought that the other aspects of healing are less important. Indeed, love is such a fundamental part of the healthy person that whatever ministry enables people to be sure of themselves and their acceptance in God's sight is as important a ministry of healing as any.

The part played by the whole Christian community in this ministry of love is very significant. It is also true that some forms of healing prayer focus on releasing the sense of this love within the person being prayed for.

AREAS OF CONTROVERSY

The areas of Christian controversy about the healing ministry are many. Disagreements concerning the basis for the ministry in the instructions Jesus gave to his disciples are discussed in depth in Chapter 4.

Concerning the Expectations of Healing Ministry

Some would say that we are still to expect astonishing events of power as in the ministry of Jesus and the apostles, as normal in the mission of the Church. Others would say that in Scripture miracles only appear at certain particular moments of the history of God's people and therefore belong to specific purposes of God at specific times. The normal and realistic expectation, therefore, should not be to hope for results outside the normal pattern of medical expectations.

Both groups would say firmly that healing 'signs' are acts of God's sovereignty and cannot be programmed by Christians. Nevertheless, there is a marked difference in the two groups as to expectations of an unusual or supernatural outcome through particular occasions of the laying on of hands. Since faith is important in relation to the healing God gives, a weak expectancy is thought by those who are hopeful for healing to be counterproductive. The reply would be that such expectancy is not well-founded, that the history of the Church shows such works to be occasional and that God will sovereignly give such healings when he chooses.

In practice, both Christian doctors and ministers make judgements about what to expect God to do when advising their 'clients'. Some Christian doctors say prayers with their patients, as do Christian ministers with those who come to them. The pitfalls are similar. Prayer is not a problem if it is for God to do what would be normal in the circumstances. Prayer that looks for God to do the exceptional needs care by either doctor or minister. False expectations can easily be generated and then disappointed. This hardly seems God's intention. A doctor praying in such a way may be misheard as giving a hopeful medical prognosis. If prayer is going to be offered it is safer if it calls upon God to heal, (or to come, if healing is unrealistic), with his power or his presence. It can be done with a strong sense of expectancy while avoiding too clear a definition of what may or may not happen.

Different expectations arising from different understandings of suffering give rise to a lot of concern. Those who emphasize healing ministry are open to criticism that their approach is simply 'triumphalism'.

Firstly, it is argued, they minimize the positive benefits which God works through pain; in other words, they have no theology of suffering. It is not hard to see how this happens. If those who are the ministers wish to emphasize the healing blessings available now from Jesus, they will feel that to stress the blessings through pain will reduce motivation for seeking healing from Christ and their faith that Jesus, does heal today.

Behind this tension is the question of whether the illness is viewed as given by God or the work of the enemy, Satan. Those who are cautious about healing ministry and stress the value of suffering are open to the criticism that they treat sickness too readily as God-given or just the way things are in a fallen world. The alternative point of view sees the battle of the kingdoms and sickness as belonging to the oppression of the enemy. It should not be accepted too readily as God-given, but be fought for in prayer.

Neither side would want any dualism here. Anything that Satan does he only does under the sovereignty of God. But there is a great art in the interpretation of any disorder in whether it should primarily be considered as an act of God, with his purpose in view, or of Satan, in his opposition to all that is good, or as a consequence of human responsibility, since God has made us as free agents, or simply the outworking of a fallen world.

Secondly, those who emphasize healing are open to the charge that they fail to do justice to the New Testament emphasis on God working through our weakness and vulnerability. Power is not such a popular concept among some Christians at present; it has such connotations of misuse. We prefer to emphasize that God's strength is made perfect in weakness.

It is clearly difficult in practice to hold together the biblical truths relating to sickness, healing, suffering and death. There is the truth that the body is subject to continual decay, with the material creation. There is the truth that God's strength is found in our weakness. There is also the truth that Jesus, in his compassion, has brought us a fullness of life, a Kingdom of God's goodness which he demonstrated as including physical healing. There is no sign of any awkward tension between these two truths in the New Testament either in relation to Jesus' ministry or the life and teaching of St Paul. It seems that the early Christian communities could live with both truths without either one denying the other.

Concerning the Context and Methods of Healing Ministry

Strong emphasis on the ministry of healing as integral to the pattern of evangelism which Jesus taught his followers always brings out the counter argument that it was preaching and not healing which he made a priority. The great commission only mentions preaching and teaching, unless the phrase 'teaching them to observe all that I have commanded you' is taken to include healing (see Chapter 4). Jesus says that he must move on to other towns to preach the Kingdom of God because this was why he was sent (Luke 4.43). But the other point of view is that his model of proclaiming the Kingdom had healing as an integral part of it.

If emphasis is placed upon a church healing ministry with laying on of hands as a prominent part of the Church's proclamation, the criticism is made that the supernatural aspects of healing ministry are overemphasized to the neglect of healing through natural means, such as medicine, counselling, psychiatry, community projects, and spiritual means such as confession, etc. The criticism is often justified and needs to be taken note of by churches in which there is a prominent focus on ministry of prayer for healing.

On the other hand, in support of a focus on prayer with laying on of hands, it may be necessary for churches to give it emphasis in order to gain a hearing for a world-view that allows the unexpected, maybe supernatural, action of God. The world-view that has won the day in western society for the past 100 years or more has allowed no place for the supernatural. In many other parts of the world, however, divine action outside what is normal is not ruled out.

Some forms of Christian ministry in which healing is prominent are wide open to the charge of sensationalism. Those doing this ministry would reply that when Jesus was doing his ministry with integrity the results were so astonishing that reports about it spread very rapidly. The problem seems to be that some present-day practitioners appear deliberately to play up the supposed miraculous nature of the cures. There is no evidence of Jesus doing this, rather the opposite.

Concerning the Results of Healing Ministry

Very frequently claims are made that God has healed, claims which turn out not to stand up to rigorous investigation.

Since Christians do not believe in a 'God of the gaps' but in a God who is active in all healing, it is not surprising that Christians who experience healing for themselves, or for others, that they did not expect, speak of God healing them. Where such testimony brings the Church into disrepute is when the claim implies that a miracle has happened contrary to the normal process of medical or natural healing but the evidence does not bear this weight. Christians should be very careful here to speak with complete integrity. People in our society will not readily understand that God is to be given the credit if there is clearly another plausible explanation.

There is also a problem when people feel better, but, in fact, are not. On the basis of their feelings they claim that God has healed them. It is easy to think one is healed because, for example, morale is improved. Christian integrity again calls for an honest account of the facts.

It is argued that although there are healings through Christian prayer ministry these are of a lesser order than the 'miraculous' healings recorded in the New Testament. Healings of the latter kind do not happen today, it is said; if they did there would be something to shout about.

Others would say that such astonishing healings are happening today, following reports that come from non-western countries. It is difficult to substantiate the claim or disprove it. Many accounts of such things are circulated. Some would say that there is a connection between the incidence of such healings and the faith and expectancy in the Church and community.

Biblical Models and Current Practice

Any attempt to simplify the diversity of approaches to the Church's healing ministry will be inadequate. We offer some models, highlighting key factors. The models are not exclusive and any particular practice of healing ministry frequently draws on more than one of them.

HEALING BY NATURAL MEANS

Key principle: Use of medicine and disciplines of counselling, psychoanalysis or other therapy. This may be done in the context of a praying church or community.

The Church has a long tradition of involvement in medical healing to which the medical missions are a clear witness. All that God has given is to be used sensibly as a resource for healing. Timothy was told by the apostle Paul to take a little wine for his stomach condition.

THE 'DISCIPLE' MODEL

Key principle: Seeking to model our ministry on the way Jesus did it. Several features of this approach are believed to follow from the principle (see also Chapter 4).

Healing in the Context of Announcing the Kingdom and Evangelism

In the mission on which Jesus sent his disciples during his lifetime, he instructed them to announce the Kingdom of God and heal the sick. This was the pattern he himself followed (Matthew 4.23; 9.35—10.8). Do the passages read as if the healing is all of a piece with the arrival of the Kingdom? If so, the Kingdom includes healing, among other things. But some are not persuaded of the integral connection.

The Kingdom of God is here in Jesus, but it is not fully present. We await the day of its fulfilment. Healing now, therefore, must be incomplete, just as we are not yet without sin even when the grace of God has worked in us deeply.

Jesus urged people to repent and believe the gospel (Mark 1.15) The healing was practical 'good news' for those who were being called to faith. Sadly the Church has all too often kept the gifts of the Spirit for itself. This model suggests that healing is not to be restricted to believers but used in reaching out to people everywhere in the power of God. In western society, however, most people are not faced with pronounced needs of physical healing, because of medical advances. The practical 'good news' of the Kingdom may therefore lie in other directions.

Compassion

As well as being part and parcel of evangelism, the healings of Jesus are born out of compassion for people who are suffering (Matthew 9.35, 36). We believe that he has the same compassion today.

Authority

Faced with the need for more workers to bring in the harvest of those who were seeking the blessings of the Kingdom, Jesus gave to the twelve disciples authority to do exactly what he was doing himself, extending his ministry fully through his disciples (Matthew 9.35—10.8). It is likely that after the resurrection the disciples still considered that they had this authority. The case for believing that this same authority is given to all Christian disciples today is considered in Chapter 4.

Method

Such evidence as we have about the way the disciples practised the healing ministry entrusted to them indicates that they did it just as they had seen Jesus do it, i.e. with firm commands or statements of authority and the laying on of hands using the name of Jesus as their authority and the source of their power (Acts 3.6, 7; 9.32–43). There is one reference to them using anointing with oil (Mark 6.13).

This model is essentially non-formal and suited to ministry in homes and public places as well as in non-formal settings in church services.

If it is true that Jesus has given authority to every Christian to act on his behalf in healing the sick it is a serious shortcoming in the history of the Church that we have been so negligent in following the instructions we have been given. If, on the other hand, this authority has not been given there are equally sad situations which have arisen through false expectations of healing.

THE 'ELDERSHIP' MODEL

Key principle: Ministry exercised by recognized elders in the local church, in the context of pastoral care and oversight.

This model derives from the well-known passage in James 5.13–16. A great many churches follow a practice along these lines. Other marks of this ministry mentioned in this passage may be followed by a greater or lesser degree. They are:

- the elders are called for, suggesting a serious condition. Presumably this does not rule out the elders offering to come;
- sacramental oil may be used;
- confession of sin and forgiveness is part of the ministry;
- the prayer is called 'the prayer of faith' and its effectiveness linked to the righteousness of the intercessor.

HEALING IN THE CONTEXT OF THE LOCAL CHURCH MEETING

TOGETHER

Key principle: Healing ministry takes place when the Church is gathering for praise and teaching.

It seems entirely appropriate to pray for personal healing when the Church meets for worship. Worship is like breathing to the Christian; it is our lifeline. When we are worshipping we are acknowledging what is fundamentally true between us and our Maker. It is the time when we place ourselves in the right relationship with God, not in rebellion, but in worship. We are expressing our total dependence upon him.

In that right relationship, God is able to restore to us the blessings which we were created to enjoy. As we allow him to rule over us, so he gives himself freely to us. His presence is at the same time the power of his Kingdom. Healing, forgiveness and all the blessings of the Kingdom are available to us.

Many churches have healing ministry available in some services and healing may be the focus of the service as a whole, i.e. a healing service. Liturgical and non-liturgical, sacramental and non-sacramental patterns may be used.

In 1 Corinthians 12.4–11, spiritual gifts are discussed and 'gifts of healings', are mentioned. In the light of the context from chapter 10 to chapter 14, which is repeatedly dealing with the conduct of worship meetings, it is probable that Paul envisages spontaneous charisms of healing given during the worship. The plural 'gifts of healings' reminds us that we are not dealing with a person who has a gift of doing healing, but rather with healings given through a believer, the gifts being the healings given to whoever the recipients are.

THE SACRAMENTAL MODEL

Key principle: The healing is given accompanying a sacrament or sign, along with prayer and perhaps laying on of hands.

There is difference among Christians about the significance of signs used in Christian worship and ministry such as baptism, Holy Communion, (Lord's Supper, Eucharist, Mass), laying on of hands, anointing with oil. This is not the place for a full discussion of such signs. Baptism and Holy Communion are usually given a distinctive place as institutions of Christ, through which gospel truth is proclaimed and its benefits received by faith. The others have a more varied use in Scripture and seem to convey meaning and grace in situations of considerable diversity.

Holy Communion proclaims the Lord's death and his coming Kingdom, which will be the completion of everything. Since the cross is where Satan was defeated, it is where healing is won by Christ. The disorder and oppression of the enemy's hold have been destroyed. There is something appropriate and powerful about doing healing ministry in close association with the celebration of Holy Communion.

Anointing with oil is used in healing several times in the Scriptures. It was believed to have medicinal effect. Oil was used in the Old Testament period for anointing kings, priests and prophets, as a sign of the Spirit of God setting them apart for their ministry. The use of oil in the New Testament for healing is therefore not just for its natural medical properties but as a sign of the power of God touching someone's life and calling them to serve.

Practical Appendix

Choosing and Training a Healing Team

If it is Christ's commission to all disciples to heal why should only some members of a church be selected to do this ministry?

People respond to Christ's call in different ways. Since participating in the ministry of healing is still unfamiliar to most church members it is most easily introduced to a church by training those who are committed to the idea. Some will then gain confidence by seeing others doing it and perhaps by their own experience of receiving healing. In the course of time it can become normal for most members of a church to be involved, at least to some extent, with prayer for healing.

Here, from experience, are some steps for developing a healing team.

STRONG COMMITMENT

To launch healing ministry effectively one's own commitment to it must be very clear. It is my experience that Satan attacks the development of this ministry more than any other that I have tried to launch, perhaps because it is a powerful and effective witness to the love of God and his availability today.

TEACHING THE CHURCH

When healing ministry is being introduced a local church must understand what is being done and why. A teaching series on healing can be very helpful, done at the main service, and perhaps, developed further in midweek teaching. The biblical basis should be covered and ways of implementing the ministry discussed. A positive partnership with medicine and psychiatry should be stressed and difficult issues addressed.

To meet the charge of triumphalism it is wise to deal carefully with the fact of incomplete healing after prayer and God's purpose in suffering and weakness. Neither in the teaching of Jesus or Paul is there any tension between the healings of the Kingdom, on the one hand, or the place of vulnerability and weakness, on the other. Yet today many Christians seem unable to affirm both confidently. When we did our first teaching series on healing at Holy Trinity, starting in January 1983, I broke my ankle in February and by Easter we had five people on crutches!

CHOOSING THE TEAM

This needs great care as some of the most eager people are those who will bring the ministry into disrepute if allowed to be the church's chosen representatives. It is important to avoid immature people, those who cannot keep confidences, those who have a problem with authority figures and those who will not be able to take criticism.

If the church leader is in a good pastoral relationship with these folk those who are not suitable for the church team can be guided as to the appropriate ministry for them. It is necessary to be very firm. Those who take on this ministry in a church must be humble people who are really good learners. If people are prickly about the decision to exclude them that illustrates their problem.

TRAINING THE TEAM

A starting point for the team is to get together those who indicate that they are drawn to this ministry and teach them, modelling in front of them how to do it. Let them see the laying on of hands, the prayer for the Holy Spirit to come, the prayer for Christ to be present and heal, or whatever words are considered appropriate. There can be teaching about the use of oil in anointing and about when and when not to touch a person. It is helpful if the meetings have a workshop style: those present can begin to practise with each other in pairs or in small groups. There are many good tapes available which can be used for training; in the end, however, there has to be the courage both to start practising and to do the teaching.

LAUNCHING THE TEAM

If the ministry is beginning in the regular services, the congregation must be told clearly when the team is available to pray and where. The confidentiality of the ministry must be emphasized. Teams need clearly appointed leaders who assign those coming for ministry to those who will pray for them. At Holy Trinity we usually had two leaders so that they could confer. It is helpful if those praying are in pairs, a man and a woman can be helpful, but some problems cannot be shared with the opposite sex. If the ministry is done often, e.g. weekly, it soon becomes normal in the church and the team learn quickly. Some churches, however, prefer a monthly provision of healing ministry.

TEAM LEARNING

In the early stages the team must be very carefully supervised, not in a critical way, but to give encouragement and guidance and to prevent bad practice developing. In our main Sunday morning service we were fortunate in having sufficient staff to be able to allocate one of the clergy to work with the healing team while another led the end of the service. It is helpful to gather the team together immediately after a ministry time to discuss questions and difficulties while they are fresh in the mind. Prayer together after (or before) the ministry is valuable. Confidentiality is a problem in team discussion and needs great care. If team members are perplexed about the way forward in a particular ministry they may need to ask permission from the one receiving the ministry to share the problem, and this may be only with the minister or team leader privately.

Learning comes by doing. At Holy Trinity we found it very valuable, and exciting, to offer weekends sharing what we were learning with other churches. To be able to concentrate on healing for a whole weekend was the best means of growth in the ministry. Faith seems to grow at such weekends and God often does lovely things in people's lives.

A monthly team meeting for longer teaching, sharing and prayer was about right. It is good for those times to include healing for individuals in the team so that what they are seeking to bring to others they are constantly receiving themselves.

INTERPRETING THE RESULTS

As the practice of healing ministry develops, wherever possible the results should be shared honestly with the congregation and interpreted. Trust will be built up not by making out that all is plain sailing but by honest evaluation of both the blessings and difficulties. It is important to emphasize that we cannot heal anyone, nor can we programme God to order. We are not Jesus and the Kingdom of God has not yet fully come. Every prayer for healing is a spiritual power struggle with the disorder of the enemy's kingdom. Our faith is weak and a climate of unbelief even affected what Jesus himself was able to do (Mark 6.5, 6)

Services of Prayer and Healing

ADAPTING REGULAR SERVICES

Churches which use regular orders of service, based upon Scripture readings, find that they can adapt these to include healing ministry. For example, the sermon can be preached after the readings, and then time which might otherwise be given to intercessions is used for the healing ministry. In any church which has a regular form of service the question to be asked is, 'At what point in the service should the ministry of healing take place and what should be omitted to make space for it?'.

We began this way at Holy Trinity, Coventry, where I was vicar from 1981 to 1992. At an evening service from the Book of Common Prayer we followed the sermon with a hymn and then invited people to come to the front to receive laying on of hands. The whole congregation was encouraged to be active in praying for those who came forward and to see what was going on as their ministry as much as that of those doing the laying on of hands. The choir sang during the time of ministry. The laying on of hands was administered in pairs, one ordained with one lay person. We chose people in good standing and with indications that they might be suited to this ministry. This 'safe' start helped to make the ministry acceptable and there was a good response after the first one or two had found the courage to come forward.

I noticed straight away that older members of the congregation, who had been at the church for many years, came forward for ministry. Not all the changes I was making were pleasing these folk, but there seemed to be no problem at all with healing ministry. It was almost as though they had been waiting for it for years.

It is my experience that most ordinary members of the churches do not find a problem with healing ministry. If they believe in God at all, (and the days are over when many went to church because it was the thing to do), people are disposed to believe that he wants to heal them and that what Jesus did 2,000 years ago is available today, at least in some measure.

It is with the professionals and semi-professionals where the doubts chiefly lie: the doctors, other professional carers, clergy, lay preachers and the like. Their study, experience and professional viewpoint all serve to raise important questions and doubts about the simplicity of faith cited above.

If the ministry continues for some time the atmosphere, far from becoming restless, seems rather to build up and God calls more and more people to respond. This may be explained in part in terms of emotion in a large gathering. On the other hand, focusing upon the work of the Holy Spirit in such a specific and personal way with those being publicly prayed for releases the work of the Spirit all over the congregation.

In a service of Holy Communion the laying on of hands can be done: (i) in place of the intercessions along the lines above while the congregation support in prayer; (ii) at the Communion rail at the same time as people receive Communion or immediately after; (iii) at some place in the church which people who wish ministry go to immediately after receiving Communion; (iv) after the distribution of the sacrament as in (i); (v) at the end of the service at some specified place: Communion rail, side chapel, front of church, etc. Endless variations are possible.

At Holy Trinity the normal Sunday morning procedure was for people to make their way to seats in a side aisle immediately after receiving Communion. The ministry team was waiting there. The ministry continued during Communion, the closing parts of the liturgy and after the end of the service. On special occasions people were asked to indicate from their seats that they wished to be prayed for and the team was sent to them. Over the years most people came to be less self-conscious about asking for prayer but it was important not to do this publicly too often.

THE LITURGICAL HEALING SERVICE

Many churches using traditional forms of liturgy have written a liturgy for a healing service. This form may then be used midweek or on Sundays for services advertised as healing services. One example written by Christopher Hamel Cooke for St Marylebone follows the following order:

- Opening sentence
- Thanksgiving and praise

- Intercession
- Readings and silence
- Address
- Confession
- Laying on of hands, sometimes with anointing
- Absolution
- Lord's Prayer
- Blessing

(Hymns are suitably positioned)

THE NON-LITURGICAL HEALING SERVICE

There can be a simple framework involving hymns or songs, a reading, a talk, confession of sin and the declaration of forgiveness, intercession for sick people not present, and ministry to those who wish to receive it. The parish of St Margaret's, Aspley, in Nottingham developed a very effective ministry to a local authority estate through a Wednesday evening healing service along these lines. The service became well-known, its worship style was accessible to those who were not familiar with Anglican services. Its success bears out the claim that people will come to church today for healing more than for any other reason.

Another pattern is used by the Provost of Coventry Cathedral, John Petty, in services held three times a month in one of the cathedral chapels. He used the same pattern in his Manchester parish in an urban priority area. While it is a service, it is designed to be mostly in silence and quite unlike usual church services.

An introduction and explanation of what is to happen are given. The minister says that we look for:

Stillness of body: a simple relaxation exercise.

Tranquillity of mind: with eyes closed, fill the mind with light.

Peace of the spirit: and we start to pray.

A prayer of *praise* is said by the minister, followed by a prayer of *thanksgiving*. In silence everyone *confesses* their sins and the minister says the words of *absolution*.

This is followed by a time of *individual* prayer. A chair is placed at a central point. One by one people take the chair and others lay hands on them. The leader says, 'We pray for *x*.' After a time of silence, the leader says, 'Thank you, Lord.'

Then there is a time of prayer for *others*. People call out a person's first name and where they are: 'Bill in Oxford.' There is a pause followed by 'Thank you, Lord.'

This service is usually taken with numbers of around twenty to thirty people and is unthreatening and quiet in style. Confession is stressed as the way to clear our relationship with God so that he can do what he wills. There is a stillness with a sense of the presence of God. Nothing is said about the nature of anyone's condition. So that numbers do not become too large, those who would come are asked to book beforehand. Personal private healing and counselling frequently arise from involvement with these healing services; a counselling team is being developed at the cathedral to follow through the ministry. Many come to these services who are not regular churchgoers; some become regular worshippers.

Choosing How You Do It

It is obviously wise to choose a way of doing healing ministry which will suit the tradition of the church and people's expectations. If the pattern is threatening this is likely to be counter-productive. If the healing service is held at a time when there was no previous service it is easier to introduce a new style to the church. On the other hand, the main congregation may then be bypassed and this does not make for growth in the whole church family.

There are many variations possible in the pattern of prayers that accompany the laying on of hands. The choice may depend upon numbers seeking ministry. Here are some alternatives:
(a) A simple liturgical prayer, the same for everyone; those receiving prayer do not describe their condition. Example (St Marylebone):

> May God who made you make you whole
> as he would have you be,
> in the name and through the power
> of the Risen and Ascended Christ,
> present with us now in his Holy Spirit.

> May he send you forth,
> renewed and restored to do his will,
> to your benefit, in the service of others,
> but above all to the glory of his Holy Name. Amen.

When anointing is used the prayer is as follows:

> As outwardly and with sacramental oil
> your body is anointed
> so may Almighty God, our Father,
> inwardly anoint your soul, to strengthen you
> with all the comfort and the joy
> of his most Holy Spirit,
> and to loose you from all that troubles you
> in body, mind, or spirit.
> May he send you forth,
> renewed and restored to do his will,
> to your benefit, in the service of others.
> but above all to the glory of his Holy Name. Amen.

(b) A brief statement by the person receiving prayer, followed by a short prayer, liturgical or extempore. Those who are ministering must be given clear instructions; some will tend to pray for far too long.

(c) The person receiving prayer shares their need, and a few questions may be asked by the ministers. The prayer time may be a little more extended, or quite extended, depending on the numbers responding, the size of the ministry team and the time available.

Ministry can be received kneeling, sitting or standing. It can be helpful to vary the position used. Body positions are important because of the attitudes they encourage: kneeling emphasizes penitence; standing stimulates alertness and a sense of expectancy. No position should be used which creates discomfort or indignity for the person receiving prayer.

Conclusion

This chapter and appendix have indicated that there is a great variety of practice among Christians who are praying for healing, and this is only drawn from the experience of a few people. As the

Church continues to develop this ministry it is clearly important that those practising healing ministry be willing to listen to, and learn from, others involved in such ministry, and those who have critical things to say, so that good and wise practices prevail and unhelpful practices are discarded.

CHAPTER 3

What Is Health?
Towards a Christian Understanding

___

Prof. Duncan Vere
Revd Dr John Wilkinson

Discussions can sometimes be frustrating, and even breakdown, simply because the people involved are using the same words, but giving them different meanings. This is a potential problem with regard to the word 'health'. It is therefore important to clarify what we mean by this term. In this chapter two senior doctors who have a good knowledge of the discussions that have gone on both within the medical community and within the Christian Church address this issue.

Health is a subject about which everyone talks without really defining what they mean, and so people often use the word in different senses without being aware of doing so. It is important, therefore, to look at what people mean when they speak about health. However, as the meanings are unfolded it will be useful to ask whether they represent something that really exists, or arise from a misunderstanding of a complex subject.

A General Definition of Health

When the Charter of the United Nations was first drawn up it included no mention of health. However, before it was signed at San Francisco in 1945 the delegate of Brazil successfully proposed that the word 'health' should be inserted into the Charter. At that time no attempt was made to define what health was, but it was clear that if the subject was to be included among the responsibilities of the United Nations it had to be defined. When, therefore, the World Health Organization (WHO) was set up in 1948 the following definition was formally adopted:

Health is a state of complete physical, mental and social well-being and not merely the absence of disease or infirmity.[1]

This definition was significant because it was found to be acceptable by the representatives of all the fifty-two founder nations of WHO, even though they held different religious and philosophical views.

The WHO definition has been criticized as being too idealistic. This is an unfair criticism for it was intended to clarify the objective of the Organization, namely, 'The attainment by all peoples of the highest possible level of health'.[2] In order to do this it had to express the ideal of the kind of health which it sought to achieve. It is, however, an ideal which WHO has often had to adapt to the particular situations of people, place and time in which it has operated.

There are two features of the definition which should be noted:
1. It reminds us that health is not a purely physical phenomenon confined to the body, but includes the mind and the society in which people live. In 1984 WHO recognized that there was also a spiritual dimension to health and invited its members to consider including this dimension in their health-care planning.[3]
2. The definition is both positive and negative. It regards health as 'not merely the absence of disease or infirmity'; that is its negative aspect. It also defines health as the presence of complete well-being in all areas of life; that is its positive aspect.

The Organization added another aspect to its understanding of health when it introduced the programme 'Health for all by the year 2000'. The title of this programme has become the official target for WHO member states. However, this title implies that health is within the gift of WHO and its members, which is patently untrue. The members of the Organization can provide health-care services for their people and can improve their accessibility to the people, but they cannot give their people health. In other words, the title confuses *health* with *health care*. As a result the title of the programme is misleading and unfortunate because it defines a target which is not achievable, however desirable that target might be.

If we reduce the WHO definition of health to its simplest terms, we find that it tells us that health is complete well-being in all areas of life. In one word, health is *well-being*, a statement with which everyone would agree. However, this leaves unanswered the question of what we mean by well-being. This is where the definition fails us, for basically it tells us something which we already knew, namely, that health is well-being.

Well-being is, of course, only one of several words in popular English speech which are used to describe what we mean by health. So let us begin our quest for the meaning of health by examining some of these words.

Health in Popular Speech

The word well-being itself, and the idea of health as 'being well', have a long history.

- Sargon II, the Assyrian conqueror of the northern kingdom of Israel in 721 BC, prayed to his gods that he might be granted: 'Length of days, fitness of body, joy of heart and radiance of spirit'.[4] This is a good description of the components of the well-being of a human individual.
- The Roman lawyer and satirist Juvenal gives another good description of it when he advises his readers to pray for 'a sound mind in a sound body' (*mens sana in corporo sano*).[5]

A concern for the well-being of other people can be illustrated by the greetings which have been traditionally exchanged between people as they meet one another. This is true of many languages both ancient and modern, but we will confine our examples to English.

- To 'salute' a person is literally to wish them good health (*salus* in Latin) and so when we meet someone we may say, 'How are you? I hope you are well.'
- If we say 'Good morning' to anyone we are wishing them a *good* morning.
- The traditional parting word, 'Farewell' is short for 'Fare you well', i.e., 'May it go well with you.'

What, then, do we mean by well-being? In fact, we all have our own idea of what constitutes well-being, but often find it difficult to put into words. As the popular saying has it, 'It's better felt than tellt'. However, it is only as we are able to reach a consensus view on what constitutes well-being that we can hope to frame an adequate and acceptable definition.

If we turn to the Oxford English Dictionary for further help in our quest, we find that the first definition of the meaning of the word 'health' given there reads as follows:

> Soundness of body: that condition in which its functions are duly and efficiently discharged.[6]

Therefore, the second word we may use to describe health is *soundness*. This in turn is defined as being 'free from disease, infirmity or injury', or in one word 'flawless'. The word 'sound' is probably related to an Old English word meaning 'strong', i.e. having the capacity and the ability to discharge its functions efficiently. It may also be related to the Latin word *sanus* which we met in the quotation from Juvenal and is the origin of the English words 'sane' and 'sanitary'.

When we inquire about the origin of the word 'health' itself we discover a third word which can be used to describe its nature. The word health comes from the Germanic root *hal* which basically means 'whole' and is the origin of the English words 'whole', 'holy', 'hale' and 'hail', all of which describe the ideal condition of a person. From this point of view, health is *wholeness*, the quality or condition of being whole, of being complete. This word in itself counters any understanding of health which is purely physical, or which concerns only one aspect of someone's total being; it introduces an idea which is often described as 'holistic' when health is discussed.

Another word which may be used for health is suggested by the reference above to the due and efficient discharge of function. This is the word *harmony*, which expresses the idea of health as a state of balance or equilibrium between the forces and functions of the human body or person. In modern medicine it is recognized that there are set ranges of hormones and other biochemicals within which body systems can function, but without which illness ensues.

Health in Popular Ideas

Because words are used to express ideas, and the ideas are reflected in their usage, we must examine the use of the words we have just discussed in order to determine the ideas about health which they represent.

First there is the idea that health is a property of life. Only where there is life can there be that wholeness, integration and harmony of being, function and relationship which is the essence of health.

Second, the standard dictionary definitions of health show that when most people speak of health today they usually mean physical health, the health of the body. As a result health tends to be measured in physical terms such as work capacity, athletic performance, biochemical blood levels or blood pressure.

A third idea is that health is simply freedom from disease and infirmity. Accordingly, a person who has no symptoms of disease is healthy. The cynic may say that when someone claims to be free from disease, it simply means that the person's physical and mental condition has not been thoroughly investigated! The WHO definition specifically extends the meaning of health beyond this negative idea.

Fourth, health is often seen as an end in itself. Many people believe that their main aim in life should be to achieve and maintain a state of physical fitness. This desire for health for its own sake is what is called 'healthism'.

Fifth, health is generally regarded as an individual matter, because it is seen as a subjective feeling of well-being. A common view is that an individual who feels well, looks well, eats well and sleeps well, *is* well. As a result, health is thought of in purely individualistic terms.

A sixth idea is that health is a human right, and so everyone is entitled to demand health as their right as human beings. In fact, health is not included amongst the human rights set out in the Universal Declaration of Human Rights adopted by the United Nations in 1948. However, the attainment of health was stated to be a human right in the WHO 1948 constitution and in 1978 this claim was made more specific in the Declaration of Alma-Ata which was adopted at a WHO/UNICEF conference on primary health care. The first article of this Declaration stated: 'The Conference strongly reaffirms that health . . . is a fundamental human right'.[7] This raises the question of whose responsibility it is to grant this a right.

A seventh idea is a revival of ancient ideas about nature; that health can be regained by recourse to the natural forces within and around us, and by regaining a lost harmony with them. This assumes that health is natural, and is lost when people move out of harmony with nature. Much of the 'New Age' ideology follows such lines.[8] If, as seems implicit in New Age thought, the only valid source of truth is our own experience, then it follows that if I believe that I experience health, I am healthy.

Finally, we should notice that in western popular thought, health has no necessary connection with religion in general, nor with Christianity in particular. This is the implication of several of the ideas above, notably that health is really a physical matter and not a spiritual one, and that health may be regarded as an end in itself. This latter idea, which we have called 'healthism', may become a substitute for true religion so that men and women may spend their lives seeking only physical perfection instead of the full development of their whole being. This is not true of eastern religions, especially Buddhism and yoga, where health and healthy living do form a joint interest within religious thought, an emphasis closely allied with the New Age thought.

The ideas we have just mentioned are very common and are often held without any realization that they are not valid in themselves but only as they express a particular world-view. When we study the meaning of health, we soon come to realize that our understanding of health is determined in general by the assumptions of our world-view, which are often unrecognized and undeclared, and in particular by our view of the nature, constitution and destiny of human beings.

Health in Medical Thinking

Doctors often hold many of the ideas that we have just suggested are prevalent in popular thought. Doctors are trained in the recognition and treatment of disease, but do not spend much time studying health. If they are asked to define health they tend to define it in terms of the absence of disease, or the presence of physical conditions which they can measure by some agreed standard. These conditions include blood pressure, biochemical blood levels and physical or mental performance tests.

In the recent past, the body has often been regarded in medical thinking as a machine, and health seen simply as the absence of disease or disability. When disease or disability do occur the function of medicine was to deal with them much as a mechanic deals with defects in a motor car. The mechanical defects may be dealt with by surgery, biochemical defects by chemical adjustments, infections by antibiotics and other derangements and symptoms by medicines of various kinds.

In more recent times it has become increasingly difficult to regard humans as simply machines. Medicine has become psycho-somatic in its approach to health and disease, taking into account the interaction of the mind and the body. The influence of the mind on the health of the body is now well-recognized. Also many conditions which used to be regarded as purely physical are held to be multifactorial in origin. This means that they are held to be due to several factors which may be physical, mental or spiritual in nature. One result of this is that medicine is losing its monopoly in the treatment of disease in the eyes of the public, who are often turning to alternative forms of therapy for relief.

If we examine the popular, and even the medical, ideas set out above, we soon realize that they are mostly based on a secular humanist view according to which humans have an existence confined only to this life and have no need of God or religion, being entirely responsible to themselves for their life and conduct. This view is not a new one for it was expressed by the ancient Greek philosopher Protagoras in his statement that 'Man is the measure of all things'.[9] There are, however, other views of the nature and destiny of human beings, and in particular there is the biblical view which is the basis of the Christian understanding of the nature and purpose of health.

Medical science and understanding has shown much that is at variance with these popular views. Western medicine has had to recognize that someone's state of mind can and does affect their physical illnesses just as physical illness can affect the mind. And every experienced doctor must have encountered patients with a spiritual problem which affects their physical and mental states deeply. We need a concept and a language which allows us to refer to the health of the various aspects of a person together, whilst keeping that ability to avoid confusion which is the motive of those reductionist definitions of health. This approach is called *holistic*, a word which implies that it takes all the different aspects of a complex matter into discussion, while respecting their relationships within the greater whole. This can be done by talking about a series of different 'levels', always taking care to say which level is being discussed and always relating it to the whole. For example, it is possible to discuss the 'Mediterranean peoples', whilst at the same time talking about the Italian or the Greek or the North African contributions to the subject, while it would be a great mistake to describe the Mediterranean peoples by confining that description to, say, the Italians; the former account is holistic, the latter reductionist.

Also, doctors recognize 'health belief models'; which are what people expect normal health to be, and what they want from healing when they feel health has deserted them. For example, 'pain relief' may mean for one person abolition of pain, whereas to another it means making pain tolerable, or something which no longer stops their activities of normal daily living. But 'normal daily living' itself is immensely variable; it is one thing when we are young and another when we are old; it is one thing if we are musical and another if we are athletic; it is one thing if someone lives in a stately home and another if they are in prison. So health expectations and beliefs depend on culture, nurture and environment. Again, doctors are very familiar with patients who expect their body to be put right, while expecting also to continue a life of stress or immoral behaviour which made them ill in the first place. It is also well-recognized that the effects of drugs depend greatly upon what their recipient expects them to do. Hence appreciation of health depends much on expectations.

Medical research has made it very clear that health can never be regarded properly as a purely individual matter; the health of individuals depends greatly upon social factors, upon the health of communities and upon the impact that social factors have on individuals' ways of living. Health is about human function, but it is function in relation to others that matters; it has become commonplace now to refer to sick families, or communities, or environments. These are social groupings, or their effects, which have adverse effects upon health. It is clear that good clean water and air, sanitation, clean food and healthy diets do far more to remove the effects and risks of disease then medicinal therapy. And health depends in part upon families' work relationships. These concepts are now so strongly established that medical training curricula openly state that they are concerned with 'whole person medicine'.

Another significant recognition is that mental pressures can cause bodily illness. This may happen when sudden stress triggers the onset of some physical disorder to which someone is predisposed, perhaps by genetic or environmental factors. It can also happen when illness supplies an emotional 'gain' or perceived benefit. Usually such illnesses take the form of 'sickness behaviour', where someone surrounds himself or herself with the paraphernalia of illness, and behaves as if sick in body, though careful medical tests may reveal inadequate evidence of physical disorders severe enough to warrant this behaviour. In a more developed form, now uncommon in western societies, but very frequent in former times, this becomes a frank hysterical illness. The sufferer is then not aware of the subconscious motivation, but demonstrates a bewildering succession of quasi-physical disorders such as blindness, loss of speech, apparent strokes or loss of sensation, with no physical evidence of disease or of any normal emotional reaction to what could be harrowing experiences if physical. But there is abundant evidence of emotional gain from the illness, such as escape from an intolerable situation or financial benefit. Such illnesses often recover suddenly, giving an impression of miraculous cure to both the sick person and those around them. If health is a general or lasting state, the concept cannot include transient problems; one headache does not render one unhealthy. But all these notions of health are reductionist. Our minds protest at concepts of health which include them alone. There is mental as well as purely physical health. And the sociologists remind us forcefully that there is more to health than our internal physical and mental condition. That may be what doctors address, but this too is reductionist.

So we reach the notion of *wholeness*. The very word suggests not a dead structure, but a complete, dynamic, soundly integrated being. Such a person is what is pictured by the traditional English expression 'hale and hearty'.

But can this be true of someone with disability? The answer must be 'yes', since much disability is part of normal life and living. There are many healthy old people who cannot do what they once could do, just as there are innumerable healthy infants who cannot yet do what they will do. If development is healthy so is decrescence. It is healthy for a man of eighty to be unable to run up a mountain.

But again, there are problems here for the concept of health: cancers increase in incidence logarithmically once middle life is passed; the chance of colon cancer doubles for every year we live past sixty-five. This may sound unhealthy, but it can be seen as the normal biological result of fading immune surveillance within the body. Death is a normal part of living. And, if we consider that relationships are within the concept of health, most people spend their life making others ill unwittingly by such things as poor diet provision, lack of exercise, smoking. Hence health must be defined within a limit which varies amongst any human population.

Health in Biblical Words

The Bible is a book which is concerned with the well-being or welfare of humankind. It is very surprising, therefore, to find that the word 'health' only occurs about fifteen times in the thousand pages which most English versions contain. Does this mean that the Bible is not really interested in health, or does it mean that the Bible has a different understanding of health from the popular one set out above?

The Old Testament

We cannot read far into the Old Testament without realizing that it is indeed very interested in health. It may not define health in any precise way, but it describes the life and activities of healthy people and unhealthy people to illustrate what it means by health, and it prescribes the kind of lifestyle which will promote health and prevent disease.

There is another surprising thing about the Old Testament. The word 'body' occurs very infrequently in its pages, and never in the context of any theoretical discussion about health. When we consult the original language in which the Old Testament was written, we find that biblical Hebrew has no word for the whole body unless it be dead. However, it has many words denoting different parts of the body and these may sometimes be used to denote the whole body.

The word which best describes the Old Testament understanding of health is the word *shalom*, which occurs about two hundred and fifty times in its pages. The basic meaning of *shalom* is 'totality' and so this word may be translated 'completeness', 'wholeness', 'soundness', 'well-being', 'harmony' or 'prosperity'; words which describe the state of the body and being of the human person as a whole. Because harmony or freedom from strife between persons and nations is a necessary condition for well-being, the word came to have the secondary meaning of 'peace'. It is this latter word which has been traditionally used in the English versions to translate *shalom*, but unfortunately this has obscured the wider and more basic meaning of the word. This wider meaning may be expressed by saying that *shalom* denotes primarily wholeness, completeness, soundness and well-being and may be used to describe these characteristics in every sphere of life whether physical, mental or spiritual, and individual, social or national. It is therefore a word of very wide application.

The other words, which are used very infrequently for health in the Old Testament, refer more strictly to healing as the process of being restored to health, and they do not add anything to the concept of *shalom*. There is, however, one word which we may regard as describing health within the Old Testament meaning of the word, and that is the word 'blessedness'. A study of those verses, particularly in the Psalms, which begin with the words, 'Blessed is the man' will add further dimensions to the concept of *shalom* in both theory and practice, and thus of health. When we do this we find that blessedness, *shalom* and health include trust in God (Psalm 40.4; 84.12), forgiveness of sin (Psalm 32.1), and obedience to God's will (Psalm 119.1–2).

It is sometimes maintained that the words for health are always used figuratively or metaphorically in the Old Testament. It would be surprising if this were so as the Old Testament is very concerned with the health of the whole being of a person. In fact, we can only sustain the view that the use of the words for health in the Old Testament is always figurative if we understand health in a purely physical sense.

The New Testament

On turning to the New Testament we find that there are more words used for health there than in the Old, but they all derive from the different meanings of *shalom* which we found in the Old Testament. There is, however, one basic difference between the two Testaments and that is that the Old Testament tells us more about health, whilst the New Testament is more concerned with healing. However, the New Testament no doubt takes for granted the teaching of the Old about health and does not repeat it.

There are a number of words which are used in the New Testament to describe health and its various aspects. Three are the nouns 'peace' (*eirene*), 'life' (*zoe*) and 'salvation' (*soteria*), and three are the adjectives 'sound' (*hugies*), 'blessed' (*makarios*) and 'mature' (*teleios*). The fact that the New Testament is more concerned with healing, which is the restoration of a health that has been lost, is seen in the use of words such as life and salvation which imply a previous state of death or sin from which someone has to be delivered, and maturity which implies a previous state of immaturity.

Health in Biblical Ideas

In biblical terms, health is not merely a quality of life, it is life itself regarded from the point of view of its wholeness and completeness. This is illustrated by the saying of Jesus in which he stated the purpose of his coming into the world as opposed to the motive of those who come to steal the sheep. 'I have come in order that you might have life – life in all its fullness' (John 10.10 GNB).

This verse is often taken to be a definition of health. In biblical terms, life is more than existence. It is life with the quality of eternity. This is why the Bible speaks of eternal life even though for the Christian believer it begins in the world of time (1 John 5.11–12). It is the life of God himself infused into human beings, which produces that wholeness and fullness of life which is health.

It follows from what we have just said that health, which is the fullness of life, is the will of God for humans. The Bible is clear that God created human beings for fellowship with himself. This is why he created them in his own image to be like himself (Genesis 1.26). They were created healthy as he is healthy. They did not however remain healthy but rebelled against him, and their fellowship with him was broken. This fall from their high estate of fellowship with their Creator had disastrous spiritual, physical, social and environmental consequences. However, God did not leave them to be the victims of their own sin and rebellion, out of fellowship with himself and out of tune with the rest of creation. He redeemed them from their sin by sending his Son,

Jesus Christ, to die on the cross so that their sin might be forgiven and their fellowship with himself restored. It is in their fellowship with God that human beings find their true health and destiny. Their health is not based on any human 'right to health', but on the desire of God to provide them with fullness of life and wholeness of being. This he has done through Jesus Christ, his Son.

In the Bible, health is a quality of the whole human being. The human being is regarded as a whole and not divided into parts. To speak solely of the health of the body is to accept a division which does not exist in biblical thought. This is why the body is so rarely referred to separately, particularly in the Old Testament. Health extends to the whole of a person's being – body, mind and spirit. We use these terms to differentiate different aspects of our being, not to separate these aspects into different and distinct parts.

A Christian Understanding of Health

It will have become obvious from our discussion so far that the answer to the question, *What is health?*, is not an easy one. Indeed, it has been said that health, like truth, cannot be defined. That statement is clearly untrue, for if truth cannot be defined then the study of theology and the practice of law become impossible. Also, if truth cannot be defined then we cannot know if any statement is true, even the statement that truth cannot be defined! Equally, if health cannot be defined then the study and practice of medicine and the pursuit of health becomes difficult if not impossible for we cannot know if anyone is healthy.

Any adequate definition of health from a Christian point of view must seek to answer the following seven questions.

1. What is the nature of health?
2. What is the purpose of health?
3. What is the standard of health?
4. What is the source of health?
5. How is health expressed in life?
6. How is health maintained?
7. Is perfect health possible in this life?

We will consider these questions and try to come to a Christian understanding of health.

The Nature of Health

The short answer to the question about the nature of health is that health consists of the wholeness of the whole being of a person in all his or her relationships. Because of this emphasis on wholeness, the Christian view of health is often described as 'wholistic' or 'holistic'. Whilst this description is true, it is open to misunderstanding because these adjectives are also applied to views of health and practices of health care which cannot be described as Christian.

As we have already seen in our discussion, there are different facets of wholeness, each of which have their own contribution to make to the understanding of the nature of health. These different facets are expressed by the words 'soundness', 'completeness', 'perfection', 'well-being' and 'maturity'. One particularly significant word for the Christian understanding of health is the word 'salvation'.

In the Gospels the verb *sozo*, to save, is used equally of deliverance from physical disease or danger as of spiritual salvation. Thus we find Jesus saying to both the woman with the chronic haemorrhage and the woman who was a sinner, 'Your faith has saved you (*sesoken se*); go in peace' (see Mark 5.34 and Luke 7.50) This is a reminder that in Christian terms the healing of the body is never purely physical and the salvation of the soul is never purely spiritual for both are combined in the restoration to wholeness of the whole person.

In his first letter to the Thessalonian Christians the apostle Paul gives a description of the nature of health when he prays for them in the following words: 'May God himself, the God of Peace, make you holy through and through, and keep you sound in spirit, soul and body, free of any fault when our Lord Jesus Christ comes' (1 Thessalonians 5.23 REB).

In the Christian understanding health, like life and salvation, is not a right but a gift – the gift of God. Access to the services which are available in our society to provide health care and promote a healthy lifestyle may be regarded as a right, but not health itself.

These insights bear powerfully upon what we may expect of medicine. A popular misconception is that modern, powerful medicines 'make people better'. In fact, medicine, whether by drugs, surgery, vaccination or radiotherapy, simply improves the conditions for natural healing to occur. This is nowhere more obvious than when pneumonia is treated by a penicillin, a drug which can kill all the invading organisms. Recovery, including the removal of dead organisms, must then follow by natural processes, occasionally, these processes become exaggerated and then become themselves the causes of disease. Health, whether intrinsically present or regained through recovery from disease is a dynamic process, the gift of God.

The Purpose of Health

We saw above that a common view of health is that it is an end in itself; a view which we called 'healthism'. However, there is a paradox in healthism similar to the paradox of hedonism (the view that pleasure is an end in itself). The paradox of hedonism is that the more one seeks pleasure for its own sake, the less likely one is to find it. Similarly in the case of health, the more one seeks health for its own sake, the less likely one is to find it. In other words, the best way to *get* health is to *forget* it in the pursuit of some other desired objective.

The biblical view is that health is not an end in itself but a means to an end. It is a by-product not an end-product. The end or the purpose of health is the glory of God and the happiness of humans. If we love God and live to his glory then we shall find health. In the classic words of the Westminster Shorter Catechism of 1647:

Question 1: What is the chief end of man?
Answer: Man's chief end is to glorify God, and to enjoy him forever.

The purpose of health is to enable us to worship and to serve God so that we may glorify him by manifesting his glory in our lives and that we may enjoy his fellowship and his blessing. We do this because we love God who first loved us and sent his Son to reveal his love to us that we might respond in worship and service.

Again, medical experience provides many varieties of example; it is not rare to find a health fanatic who is desocialized by the pursuit of health to the point of illness, whether by idiosyncratic or frankly depressed behaviour. Some doctors became so concerned that they were not taking their own advice to patients about regular exercise, that their guilt feelings could only be expunged by wearing a pedometer. The device showed that they walked on average seven miles each day in the pursuit of their ordinary duties. As we have said, it is not rare to find patients who 'enjoy ill health' in the sense that they gain emotionally from sickness behaviour and so cease to live healthily. The purpose of health is to live; the purpose of living is not primarily to be healthy.

The Standard of Health

To speak of health as wholeness is meaningless unless at the same time we define the standard by which that wholeness can be assessed. If we speak in terms of purely physical health or fitness then we can use the standards of athletic achievement on the sports or games field and compare our achievement with that of the average or the Olympic athlete. But when by health we mean the wholeness of the whole person, and not just of the body, what standard shall we use?

Paul has no doubt about the answer to that question. In his letter to the Ephesians he speaks of 'the whole man' (*aner teleios*) as one who has attained to 'mature manhood, measured by nothing less than the full stature of Christ' (Ephesians 4.13 REB). It is worth noting that this maturity is reached through a common faith in, and a full knowledge of, the Son of God, and in the context of the body of Christ, namely, the Church (Colossians 1.28 REB) This makes it social as well as individual.

Therefore, the standard of health for the Christian is Jesus Christ himself. This means that Christians should aim at the standard of health which is exemplified by Jesus Christ and which they believe that it is Jesus' will that they should attain in all aspects of their being. In the Gospels we see how Jesus was hungry and thirsty, tired and under stress, and we may expect to have these experiences for they are part of the normal response of a healthy body and mind to situations which arise in daily life. We see how he suffered physically and spiritually and we may expect to suffer too. Indeed it could be argued that because of misunderstanding and alienation his family and social environments were decidedly unhealthy. Throughout all this he maintained a positive equilibrated and integrated health, seeking in compassion to heal others who were broken by similar environments.

What can this mean in practical terms? Jesus was clearly committed in his entire being to his Father's will; he spent himself upon making him known, upon his redemptive work, upon those who came to him in faith. This meant hard physical effort, tiredness, thirst and hunger at times, but also withdrawal from stress when this seemed needful for himself or for others. Above all, though he was the Son of God, he accepted human limitations, the confinements to time and place and the needs of his body. However, we do not know whether or not he was ever ill, or what he would have done if disabled or aged since he was neither. We know well his commitment to a healing ministry as a part, not the whole, of his profile of good works. And we know much more about the outworkings of his teachings within his 'body', the early church.

The apostles were also concerned with healing, but were often unwell. Both Paul and Timothy had chronic diseases. In Paul's case it may have been malaria or an eye infection which periodically incapacitated him (Galatians 4.13). He asked God to cure him, but instead of taking the disease away God provided an antidote to give him strength in his times of weakness (2 Corinthians 11.7–9). Timothy had frequent attacks of illness which produced a dyspepsia for which Paul prescribed the drinking of some wine (1 Timothy 5.23). Two other friends of Paul suffered from diseases which appear to have been more acute in nature. Epaphroditus of Philippi contracted an acute infection in Rome from which he nearly died (Philippians 2.25–30). Trophimus had to be left behind because he was ill when Paul left Miletus, but we are not told the nature of his illness (2 Timothy 4.20). All these suffered from ill-health, and it is important to remember that they all had colleagues to whom the Holy Spirit had given the gift of healing, yet they were not healed.

They used the medicines available to them, and also prayed for healing. At times God's gift for them might be disability (2 Corinthians 11; 12.7–9), but if so it was received as part of his grace and the enablement for better functioning as members of his 'body', the Church (2 Corinthians 12.9f.; Galatians 4.14–15; 6.11). They lived in a fallen world as those who were being shaped for something different, something better. They sought health so that they might serve (2 Corinthians 12.8), but endured health hazards too, for the same reason (2 Corinthians 4.7–11; 11.23–29). They were clearly 'whole' in body, mind and spirit in their integrated functioning in Christ's 'body', the Church of God on earth. In no sense were they miracle dependent; even those who had been raised from death later died naturally. The miracles were signs that pointed to God's power, not to permanent physical health on earth.

The Source of Health

The keyword in the answer to the question about the source of health is the word *relationship*, and more specifically a *right* relationship. The source of human health lies in having a right relationship to God, to oneself, to our neighbours, and to our environment.

First, then, the primary source of health is God and it is in a right relationship to God that humans find health and wholeness. The Bible has no doubt about what this right relationship should be. It should be one of faith and obedience; faith in God as the source of health, and obedience to his laws whether physical, moral or spiritual. The word which the Bible uses for this right relationship to God is 'righteousness' and the prophet Isaiah assures the women of Jerusalem that 'the fruit of righteousness will be *shalom*' (Isaiah 32.17).

Second, health arises from a right relationship of a person to himself or herself. Our being is the creation of God, and our life and health are gifts of God of which we are not the owners, but the stewards. We therefore have the responsibility of caring for ourselves in our whole being. Within this context, the care of our body is vitally important.

Third, health comes from a right relationship of people to one another. This relationship was defined by Jesus when he summarized our duty to our fellows in the two commandments:

Love your neighbour as yourself. (Matthew 22.39 NIV)

Do to others what you would have them do to you. (Matthew 7.12 NIV)

Fourth, health includes a right relationship of people to their environment. Humans are the stewards of creation and were made so by God. We are responsible for the care of creation. This care will in turn produce healthful conditions which will promote our own health and the health of all creation.

The Expression of Health in Life

We have already seen that health cannot be regarded simply as the absence of known disease or recognizable symptoms. It is expressed in the positive characteristics which we have already mentioned as included in the concept of wholeness. Also since the human person is a whole and not simply a sum of different parts these features of health apply to the whole of our being and not simply to one part or aspect.

The first characteristic by which health finds expression in human life arises from our relationship to God. When this relationship is right it results in holiness of character and uprightness of living. It enables a person to obey the divine command to be holy as God is holy, a command which is repeated five times in the book of Leviticus (11.44, 45; 19.2; 20.7, 26). A study of the context of these five occurrences of this command in Leviticus will soon show that the holiness in view is not some remote spiritual piousness, but a very practical quality of daily living which extends even to the hygienic disposal of excreta, as we see from Deuteronomy 23.12–14. It is interesting to notice that when Jesus gives a similar command in Matthew 5.48 he uses the word 'perfect' (*teleios*, mature, fulfilling the purpose *telos* of our existence).

The second characteristic is the peace which health brings to body, mind and spirit seen as serenity and freedom from anxiety. Health means that we need take no anxious thought for the morrow (Matthew 6.34). So we find the prophet Isaiah in the verse we have already quoted, assuring the women of Jerusalem that 'the effect of righteousness will be quietness and confidence for ever' (Isaiah 32.17 NIV).

The third characteristic is strength, by which is meant not only physical strength, but also strength of mind and spirit, strength of the whole person. Karl Barth, the Swiss theologian, defined health as 'the strength to be as man' which 'serves human existence in the form of the capacity, vitality and freedom to exercise the psychical and physical functions'.[10]

Health is therefore the strength by which we live. In his volume of Gifford Lectures, Jürgen Moltmann identified this strength as 'nothing other than love'.[11] In New Testament terms it is *grace*, the grace that Paul found was made perfect in him when the weakness of his thorn in the flesh came upon him (2 Corinthians 12.7–9).

The fourth characteristic by which health finds expression in human life is harmony. Harmony between God and humankind, within a person's being, between people, and between humans and the rest of creation. Part of this desirable situation is described by the psalmist when he writes: 'What a wonderful thing it is when brothers live together in harmony' (Psalm 133.1 AV).

The fifth characteristic is the negative one of the absence of disease, which is an important aspect of health for most people. That this is part of the biblical understanding of health can be seen from those verses in which worship of God and obedience to his commands are linked to the prevention or removal of disease. Two of these verses are found in the book of Exodus:

> Worship the Lord your God, and his blessing will be on your food and water. I will take away sickness from among you, and none will miscarry or be barren in your land. I will give you a full life span. (Exodus 23.25–26 NIV)

> If you listen carefully to the voice of the Lord your God and do what is right in his eyes, if you pay attention to his commands and keep all his decrees, I will not bring on you any of the diseases I brought on the Egyptians, for I am the Lord, who heals you. (Exodus 15.26 NIV)

Certainly it is true that careful obedience to the will of God avoids or averts much sickness. But it is essential to recognize that this is no more true of *all* illness now than it was for Israel in Old Testament times. Some people are born with an inheritance that leads to illness directly; many are disabled by sickness or accidents. It is becoming clear that even cancers may often have an inherited mechanism, at least in part of their causation. In no sense can those illnesses be avoided by godly behaviour. However, it is equally true that unhealthy diet and tobacco cause the majority of disabling or fatal illnesses in western societies, a fact with clear implications for those whose motivation is to live as a part of Christ's body as a whole. As Paul's experience as a Christian shows, wholeness is possible in the use of disability; he did not ignore disability, enjoy it or deny it, nor was he depressed by it. He was able to receive it as a thing seen to be part of God's grace for him, and to use it as an integrated part of his total 'living for Christ', and in Christ. The aim must be to live a full spiritual life using a body with its unavoidable disabilities. Sickness is then an opportunity, not the means of ill-health. It is something that, whether disability is or is not removed, can be used for God, and in that sense can be used healthily.

The Maintenance of Health

As we have already seen, health is for most people a gift given into our care at birth as a complete gift; for some who are born with serious disabilities it is partially marred, though there is still much to be conserved and cared for. As with all gifts its maintenance becomes the responsibility of the recipient and their near family. The need for such maintenance is a matter of common sense if we are to enjoy living and avoid the consequences which follow from a lack of maintenance.

Common sense, however, does not always provide an effective or adequate motive for the maintenance of health. For the Christian there are higher motives and these are the glory of God and human happiness.

There are four broad areas of human life and activity in which the maintenance is appropriate, and indeed essential, for human development and happiness. These are personal, family, social and environmental.

PERSONAL HEALTH

We live in the body in this world and our body is liable to disease and degeneration, some of which is preventable or curable. Christians have the highest motive for seeking and maintaining the health of the body for, as Paul reminds us, our bodies are the members of Christ (1 Corinthians 6.15) and are temples in which the Holy Spirit lives (1 Corinthians 6.19). We should therefore take advantage of all measures which are designed to prevent disease and promote physical health.

We need to maintain the health of our minds. We need to feed them on wholesome fare as Paul exhorts his Christian friends: 'Fill your minds with those things which are good and that deserve praise: things that are true, noble, right, pure, lovely and honourable' (Philippians 4.8 GNB).

We need also to control the exercise of our wills and the expression of our emotions by submitting them to the guidance and direction of the Holy Spirit.

We are not born spiritually healthy. This soon becomes apparent as we grow up and relate to other persons and have to make ethical decisions. These decisions often illustrate the tendency within us to choose the wrong rather than the right, as Paul found (Romans 7.19). To promote our spiritual health we need first of all to seek forgiveness of our sin by faith in Christ as our Saviour, and then claim the help of the Holy Spirit to restore and maintain our spiritual health.

Although we have followed the convenient analysis of the human being into body, mind and spirit, we must remember what we have already mentioned above, namely, that each human being is an indivisible and inseparable whole. Thus when we speak of personal human health we mean the well-being of the whole and not simply that of one part or aspect. Ill-health is never confined to one aspect of a person. There are physical, mental and spiritual consequences in every disease and disability. Even the common cold can produce marked mental and spiritual depression, and mental and spiritual depression can produce physical symptoms in the absence of physical disease.

FAMILY HEALTH

Human individuals are not created to be alone, but to be born and brought up in families. The family is the oldest of all human institutions. The maintenance of family well-being is thus an important part of the maintenance of human health. This is illustrated by the concern of the apostle Paul for proper relationships within the family, as seen in Ephesians 5.22—6.9 and Colossians 3.18–25. Family health is poor in western societies, and often seems much stronger in less affluent cultures. Advanced technologies often contribute to the breaking up of healthy families; consider the impact of transport, sport, entertainment and possessions, especially property-used-as-wealth, all elements which can be used together in healthy family life, but often serve to dissociate it when they become goals in themselves. Modern possessions can force the family to become a sacrifice.

SOCIAL HEALTH

The family is the basic unit of any society or nation and the well-being of society depends on the presence within it of both personal and family healthfulness. All members of society have an equal responsibility to seek its welfare and to respect the rights of all irrespective of race, nationality, sex or creed. Only when this responsibility is accepted and acted upon, and when all that is evil is repudiated can a society be called healthy. But the family is the basic building unit of any community, even of the state, just as it has always been of the local church.

ENVIRONMENTAL HEALTH

Humans were made the stewards of the creation and have the responsibility of caring for all parts and aspects of the world in which they live. We should avoid or control all activities which increase the incidence of disease, increase the prevalence of evil or interfere with the healthful functioning of our environment.

The Possibility of Perfect Health in this Life

We come now to reconsider the question: Is the health which we have described, completely and permanently attainable in this present life?

The answer of the Bible and of human experience to this question is clearly in the negative. Complete and permanent health might be taken to imply the absence of disability and suffering, degeneration and death and this is obviously not true of our present life. Even our understanding of the nature of health varies with age. What is healthy in the young is not necessarily healthy in the old, and vice versa. Also, the effects of ill-health are so universally present in our human life that we must conclude that perfect health is not possible for us in this life. There is no-one alive today who can honestly claim to enjoy complete and permanent well-being of body, mind, spirit, society and environment. We have seen that the same was true of the apostles and other members of the early church.

However, although it is true that we live in the midst of disease, suffering and death, for our world has been marred by sin and evil, a measure of health is attainable in this life and indeed is a necessity. We need a healthy body to resist disease, a healthy mind to resist disorder, a healthy spirit to resist evil and a healthy society to resist anarchy. But this measure of health is neither complete nor permanent.

The question, therefore, arises of when, in the Christian view, we shall be able to enjoy health which is complete and permanent. The beginnings of an answer to this question are already to be found in the Old Testament in the book of the prophet Isaiah. He looks forward to the messianic age when harmony will be restored to the animal creation (Isaiah 11.6–9), and in his description of the restored Jerusalem he says: 'No one living in Zion will say, "I am ill"; And the sins of those who dwell there will be forgiven' (Isaiah 33.24 NIV).

However, it is only in the New Testament that the question is really answered. There we are assured that we shall attain complete and permanent health of our whole being at the resurrection when the disintegration of our being which occurred at death will be reversed as our body is reunited with what left it at death. At that time we shall change our weak, dishonoured and perishable natural body for a powerful, glorious and imperishable spiritual body and take our place in the whole creation which has been formed anew by God (1 Corinthians 15.35–37; cf. Romans 8.18–25 and 2 Peter 3.11–13).

Finally, what shall we say about healing? If we can attain a measure of health in this life, this means that some healing is possible too. God has made our bodies and our minds self-healing within certain limits. Every time a surgeons operate they declare their faith in the self-healing power of the tissues of the body. They would not dare to use their scalpels unless they believed that the body would heal their incisions. Also God has put healing substances into his creation which people have discovered and we are able to use in promoting healing. Psychiatrists too can use their knowledge of how the mind is able to recover its health in certain cases to promote mental healing. In fact, medical practice is based on human discovery and use of the agents and principles of healing which God has implanted in his creation. This we may call healing on the basis of creation.

There is also healing on the basis of redemption, for through the gospel men and women can find spiritual life and health by faith in Jesus Christ who brings forgiveness of sin, power to overcome temptation and victory over death, all of which are important factors in the promotion and attainment of health.

Such healing is not complete or permanent except in specific cases and for specific diseases. In the cases of healing by Jesus in the Gospels the sick were completely and permanently healed of the particular disease they suffered from at that time, but they were not given immunity to future disease nor made immortal. They all died later of some disease or injury, and in the case of Lazarus and the Nain widow's son, they both eventually died a second time after being raised from the dead by Jesus (John 11.38–44 and Luke 7.11–15). Christian healing in this life does not, therefore, confer immunity to disease, inability to sin or exemption from death. Nevertheless, it does help us to give an answer to the problems of the existence of suffering, the meaning of death and the nature of health.

Summary

We began with the question, *What is Health*? and with the intention of seeking a Christian understanding of the nature and significance of health. Let us now summarize our findings.

Health is the complete wholeness of a person's entire being in all aspects of body, mind and spirit. This includes human relationships to God, to fellow humans and to their environment, as well as within one's own person.

Health is the gift of God, given in order that men and women may love and glorify God in their being, doing and living. The standard of health becomes that which God provided in his Son, Jesus Christ, in the senses discussed above. This does not mean that we should seek to make our lives a copy of his but rather that his attitudes, inner resource and relationship to God are the means and the model for healthy living.

Health is expressed in life by holiness of character, serenity of being, strength of body, harmony of living and absence of disease. Whilst a measure of health is possible in this life, the permanent attainment of complete health must await the resurrection. But it is right to seek it as a means to these ends.

References

1. World Health Organization, Basic Documents (WHO, Geneva 1948), p. 1.

2. Charter of the WHO, Article 1.

3. WHO Chronicle (1984), Vol. 38, No. 4, p. 172.

4. D.D. Luckenbill, *Ancient Records of Assyria & Babylonia* (University of Chicago Press 1927), Vol. 2, p. 24.

5. Juvenal, *Satire X*, line 356.

6. Oxford English Dictionary, Compact edition (Oxford University Press 1971), Vol. 1, p. 1273, s.v. 'Health'.

7. Declaration of Alma-Ata, Article I.

8. For an introduction to New Age thinking see: E.C. Lucas, 'A Short Introduction to the New Age Movement', *Science and Christian Belief*, 4 (1992), pp. 3–11).

9. Protagoras quoted by Socrates in Plato's *Theaetetus*, 152A.

10. K. Barth, *Church Dogmatics* (T and T Clark 1961), tr. H.A. Kennedy, III/2, p. 357.

11. J. Moltmann, *God in Creation* (SCM Press 1985), p. 273

Further Reading

A. Fergusson, ed., *Health: The Strength to be Human*, (CMF/IVP 1993).

J. Wilkinson, *Health & Healing: Studies in New Testament Principles and Practice* (Handsel Press 1980).

CHAPTER 4

The Significance of Jesus' Healing Ministry

Revd Dr Ernest Lucas
Dr Peter May

Christians who truly want to be disciples of Jesus will naturally turn to the picture of his ministry as it is recorded in the Gospels in order to obtain inspiration, understanding and guidance concerning their ministry today. This applies as much to the ministry of healing as to any other form of ministry. Since the Gospels make it clear that healing played an important part in Jesus' ministry, there is no shortage of material. The problem lies in assessing its significance for us today, as will become clear in the following chapter. This is written by a biblical studies scholar, who has worked as a biochemist in a medical school, and a medical doctor who is a General Practitioner with many years' experience of studying claimed miraculous healings.

Jesus' Healing Ministry

We will start with a brief survey of the nature of Jesus' healing ministry. Perhaps the first thing to note about it is the wide range of conditions with which Jesus dealt.

• Some were infections caused by micro-organisms. We read several times of Jesus healing 'lepers' (see for example, Mark 1.40–45; Luke 17.11–19). It is generally agreed that the term 'leprosy' in the New Testament covers a variety of skin conditions. The elaborate rules for isolating the sufferers show that at least some of these were contagious infections. Peter's mother-in-law's fever was presumably an infection (Mark 1.29–31).

- Some appear to have been long-standing organic disorders, e.g. the woman who had a haemorrhage for twelve years; the woman who had a bent spine for eighteen years; the man who had been paralysed for thirty-eight years (Mark 5.25–34; Luke 13.10–17; John 5.1–9). Some forms of paralysis can be hysterical rather than organic in origin, but even a long-standing hysterical condition will produce organic changes.
- In some cases the condition had existed since birth, e.g. the man born blind (John 9), or at least since childhood, e.g. the so-called 'epileptic' boy (Mark 9.14–29. In fact we cannot be sure what his ailment was.)
- There are some healings that are represented purely as exorcisms (see for example, Mark 1.23–27; 5.1–13).
- Some people were raised from the dead: Jairus' daughter; the widow of Nain's son; Lazarus (Mark 5.35–43; Luke 7.11–17; John 11).

The healings which are reported in detail seem to have been complete and instantaneous, with the exception of the 'two-stage' healing of the blind man in Mark 8.22–26. In the context of Mark's Gospel this particular healing clearly acts as a parable of the fact that the disciples receive their spiritual 'sight' in two stages. First, they recognize that Jesus is the Messiah, but their understanding of this is imperfect and they have to learn that he will suffer and die in the fulfilment of his messianic mission. Whether or not this didactic use of the healing is purely Marcan or goes back to Jesus must remain a matter of conjecture.

Jesus' healings were usually brought about by a simple word of assurance or command, e.g. 'Go your way, your faith has made you well' (Mark 10.52); 'Go; be it done for you as you have believed' (Matthew 8.13); 'I say to you, rise, take up your pallet and go home' (Mark 2.11). On some occasions we are told that he touched the person who was healed. The significance of this varied. In the case of people with leprosy (see for example, Mark 1.14) it can be seen as a gesture of acceptance to those who have been the outcasts of society, cut off from direct human contact. In other cases it may be primarily a form of communication with people for whom touch was one of their major senses, replacing a lost sense, e.g. with a deaf and dumb man (Mark 7.13–37) and blind men (Matthew 20.34). When he took the hand of Peter's mother-in-law or Jairus' daughter (Mark 1.31; 5.41) this seems to be more a gesture of command than just the 'healing touch' which it is in some other cases (see for example, Mark 6.5).

On a few occasions Jesus made use of spittle (Mark 7.33; 8.23) or clay made of spittle and mud (John 9.6). It is true that in the Hellenistic world spittle was used in magical practices and was also held to have healing properties. On this point Cranfield comments judiciously, 'There is no question of the magical use here; but whether Jesus made use of spittle simply in order to indicate to the man that he was to expect a cure and so to awaken faith on his part, or whether he also had in mind any natural effect of the spittle, it is difficult to decide'.[1]

There are several occasions when Jesus says to someone who has been healed, 'Your faith has made you well', or similar words, for example, the woman with the haemorrhage, Bartimaeus, the Samaritan leper (Mark 5.34; 10.52; Luke 17.19). We are also told that Jesus took note of the faith of those who brought a paralysed man to him, and were not easily deterred (Mark 5.34). The obverse of this is that when in 'his own country' Jesus 'could do no mighty work there, except that he laid his hands on a few sick people and healed them. And he marvelled because of their unbelief' (Mark 6.5–6 RSV).

The Significance of Jesus' Healing Ministry

The Kingdom of God

The Gospels make it clear that Jesus' ministry must be understood in the light of the concept of the Kingdom of God. Thus Mark introduces Jesus' public ministry with the words: 'Jesus came into Galilee, preaching the gospel of God, and saying, "The time is fulfilled, and the kingdom of God is at hand; repent and believe in the gospel"' (Mark 1.14–15 RSV). Matthew specifically links the healing aspect of Jesus' ministry with the preaching of the Kingdom of God, saying that Jesus went about 'preaching the gospel of the kingdom and healing every disease and every infirmity among the people' (Matthew 4.23; 9.35). The Greek word translated as 'every' has a variety of senses. Here it probably means 'all sorts of '. Three considerations point in this direction:

* the following verse in Matthew 4.24 gives a list of the various afflictions healed by Jesus;
* the fact that Jesus did not heal everyone who was sick, e.g. in Nazareth;
* the similar use of the word in Matthew 23.27.

Although the Kingdom of God was at the centre of Jesus' preaching, he nowhere gives a concise definition of the term, nor does anyone ask him to explain it. This is because the concept was not a new one for Jesus' hearers. It was available for Jesus to take up and modify for his own use. In order to understand the concept we need to look briefly at its background and its development as used by Jesus.

The expression 'the Kingdom of God' does not occur in the Old Testament. However, the idea of God as king is prominent there. In the Blessing of Moses the events at Sinai are spoken of as the moment when 'the Lord became king in Jeshurun' (Deuteronomy 33.5; 'Jeshurun' is a rare title for Israel). The prophets continually remind Israel and Judah that God is their king (Isaiah 43.15, for example). They also speak of God as king of all the earth. This follows naturally from their monotheism (Jeremiah 10.6–7, for example). The Psalms are full of references to God as the universal king (e.g. Psalm 22.28; 96.10). The emphasis in the Old Testament references to God as king is dynamic, on the fact that he rules and on the nature of that rule. Related to this is the idea of God 'visiting his people' both to deliver them from oppressors and to judge them and punish them for their rebellion against him.[2] Behind this there is the fact that God's rule is one that makes moral demands. When he became king of Israel at Sinai he gave his people a moral law.

Although God is king now, the prophets also speak of a time when he will become king and establish his rule over the earth (e.g. Isaiah 2.2–4; Obadiah 21; Zechariah 14.9). The same idea is at least implied in some Psalms (e.g. Psalm 96.10–13). So, while God is seen as king over all the earth and also, in a special way, King of Israel, his rule is only partially and imperfectly realized now. It will be fully realized at some point in the future. Events in history which are seen as demonstrations of God's rule are regarded as foreshadowing the coming of his rule in its fullness.

This applies especially to what the prophets interpreted as acts of God's judgement on nations. They sometimes, therefore, used 'end of the world' language of these events within history (e.g. Isaiah 13.9–13).

In the Jewish apocalyptic literature of the period between the Old and the New Testaments the distinction between God's *de jure* rule now and his full *de facto* rule in the future is enhanced. Sometimes this goes to the extent that 'this age' is referred to as 'the kingdom of the enemy'. In due time God will intervene to destroy the enemy and bring in 'the age to come'. In *The Testament of Dan* 6.4 the writer looks forward to 'the day in which Israel trusts' when 'the enemy's kingdom will be brought to an end'.

It was the rabbis who coined the phrase 'the Kingdom of Heaven'. 'Heaven' was used in order to avoid using the word 'God' or his name (in case they should use it in vain). Also, they tried to avoid making God the subject of active verbs. Hence by the phrase 'the Kingdom of Heaven' they meant 'God's kingly rule'. They taught that God's universal rule exists now, but will remain hidden until it 'comes' and is revealed in its fullness at the end of this age. Meanwhile it can be made a reality in the lives of individuals when they accept 'the yoke of the Law' and live by it.

Jesus understood his ministry as fulfilling the future hope expressed in the Old Testament. This is made very clear in two incidents – his visit to the synagogue in Nazareth (Luke 4.16–21) and his reply to John the Baptist's question (Luke 7.18–23). Here he claims to be fulfilling passages which speak of the character of the age that is to come after God's decisive act of salvation and judgement. This is an implicit claim that God's kingly rule is now at work in the world in a new way.

Some of Jesus' sayings make it clear that he saw the Kingdom of God as being present in power in his person and ministry. One of the most direct of these sayings is: 'If it is by the Spirit of God that I cast out demons, then the kingdom of God has come upon you' (Matthew 12.28; Luke 11.20). Another such saying is, 'The kingdom of God is not coming with signs to be observed; nor will they say, "Lo, here it is!" or "There!" for behold, the kingdom of God is in the midst of you' (Luke 17.20–21 RSV). Although some translate the last phrase of verse 21 as 'within you', the best translation of the Greek text here is probably 'in the midst of you' because this is a common meaning of the Greek preposition used here when linked with a plural noun or pronoun (in this case 'you'); and because elsewhere Jesus always speaks of people entering or being in the Kingdom, not of the Kingdom being within individuals. It is in the midst of Jesus' hearers in the person and ministry of Jesus himself.

On the other hand there are sayings of Jesus which speak of a future coming of the Kingdom. The most obvious is the petition in the Lord's Prayer, 'Your kingdom come' (Luke 11.2; Matthew 6.10). Then there is his reaction to the faith of the centurion, 'I tell you, many will come from east and west and sit at table with Abraham, Isaac, and Jacob in the kingdom of heaven, while the sons of the kingdom will be thrown into outer darkness' (Matthew 8.11–12 RSV). Although the sayings about the coming of the Son of Man in glory do not explicitly mention the Kingdom, its consummation is implied in the light of the background of the imagery in Daniel 7, where the 'one like a son of man' receives the everlasting kingdom. This link does become explicit in the parable of the sheep and the goats (Matthew 25.31–45).

Many of the parables of the Kingdom, such as those in Matthew 13, make the same point about it being present and yet, in some sense, still to come. The parables of the hidden treasure and the costly pearl speak of its hiddenness in the world now. Those of the mustard seed and the leaven make the point that it starts small, and hidden, and grows. Parables like those of the sower, the wheat and the tares and the net speak of a struggle going on in 'this age' between the kingly rule of God and the power of the evil one.

In the Old Testament the kingly rule of God is characterized by 'shalom'. This Hebrew word is usually translated into English as 'peace', but this is an inadequate translation. It refers to the situation which comes about when there is a relationship of harmony be-tween God and his creatures and between the creatures themselves. At present this harmony is disrupted by evil. The result manifests itself in moral, social, psychological and physical disorders. When God steps in to establish his rule these disorders disappear (e.g. Isaiah 9.1–9; 35.1–10; 65.17–25). It is significant that both when he forgave sins and when he healed Jesus sometimes said to people 'Go in peace' (for example: Mark 5.34; Luke 7.50). Jesus' saying about taking his yoke in order to find rest (Matthew 11.28–30) is relevant here although it does not use the word 'peace', especially since it clearly alludes to the rabbinic idea that those who take on the 'yoke of the Law' enter the Kingdom of God. In this saying 'Rest for your souls' does not mean just inner peace. 'Soul' here is probably being used in the Hebraic way as a reflexive pronoun, so that what Jesus is talking about is 'rest for yourselves (the whole person)'. The healing ministry of Jesus was part of the demonstration that the *shalom* which is the result of God's kingly rule had become a reality in the world.

The Battle with Satan

We have seen that some of the parables of the Kingdom contain the motif of a struggle between God and an 'enemy', a struggle which will not be fully resolved until the end of the age. This idea of a struggle is, of course, a theme which runs through Jesus' ministry from the temptations in the wilderness to the cross.

In the course of his ministry the struggle with Satan and the powers of evil is most obvious in the exorcisms. The significance of these is summed up in the controversy aroused by the accusation that Jesus cast out demons in the power of Beelzebul, another name for Satan (Matthew 12.22–32; Mark 3.22–30; Luke 11.14–22). Here Jesus declares that he has 'bound the strong man' and that this is evidence that the Kingdom of God has come into the world. The binding of Satan was one of the things which the Jews expected to happen only at the end of the age. This is evidenced in the following quotations from Jewish books written a century or so before the time of Jesus:

> And Beliar shall be bound by him. And he shall grant his children the authority to trample on wicked spirits. (*The Testament of Levi* 18.12; 'Beliar' is a title for Satan)

> Then his kingdom will appear throughout his whole creation. Then the devil will have an end. (*The Testament of Moses* 10.1)

Yet Jesus declares that the 'binding', or defeat, of Satan is happening in his ministry. This is emphasized in Jesus' response to the report of the seventy that they have been able to cast out demons, 'I saw Satan fall like lightning from heaven' (Luke 10.18). Their success was a sign of Satan's defeat.

Some of Jesus' healings are spoken of explicitly in terms of freeing people from Satan's power. The woman with a bent back is described by Jesus as someone 'whom Satan bound for eighteen years' (Luke 13.16). The language used in Mark 7.35 ('the bond of his tongue was loosened') suggests that, in the view of Jesus' contemporaries, what caused this man's speech difficulty was a 'binding' by a demon. The healings of Jesus, therefore, fit into the context of the confrontation that is the result of God's rule entering the world in a new way to free people from the rule of Satan, which holds people in bondage to evil. This bondage results in a variety of disorders which are the antithesis of God's *shalom*.

Compassion

What has been said so far could leave the impression that Jesus used suffering people as a means to an end. Healing them was simply a 'visual aid' to support his claim that 'the kingdom of God is at hand'. Any such idea is dispelled in the Gospels because we are told several times that Jesus' healing ministry (and indeed his teaching ministry) was also motivated by compassion when he saw the needs of people. Matthew says this twice in 'summary statements' (Matthew 9.35–38; 14.14). In other places we are told of Jesus' compassion leading him to heal specific people (for example, Mark 1.41; Luke 7.13). A distraught parent feels able to appeal to Jesus' compassion (Mark 9.22).

This reminds us that the Kingdom of God is not an abstract power but the kingly rule of a personal God. Jesus' teaching about the Kingdom cannot be divorced from his teaching about God. Jesus taught his disciples to think of God as a good father. They were to pray for the coming of the Kingdom of the one they could address as 'Our Father'. He wants to give the Kingdom to those ready to receive it (Luke 12.32–34). Some of the parables (especially those in Luke 15) depict him taking the initiative to seek out the lost. They also warn of the seriousness of rejecting God's invitation (for example, Matthew 22.1–14).

The Ministry of Jesus' Disciples

Jesus insisted that his ministry was directed to 'the lost sheep of the house of Israel' (Matthew 15.24; cf. Matthew 10.5–6).

Because he came to fulfil the Old Testament hope of Israel, God's chosen people, the gospel of the Kingdom was to be preached to them first. The nation as a whole rejected Jesus and his message, but some individuals did respond in repentance, faith and commitment to Jesus. Jesus seems to have seen them as the beginning of a new Israel, as indicated by the choice of the Twelve. Such a view of the disciples might have its origin in the concept of the righteous remnant of Israel which is found in the Old Testament prophets (for example, Isaiah 7.3; 10.20–22; Jeremiah 31.7–9). The promise given to Abraham that the nations would be blessed through his seed would find its fulfilment through Jesus' disciples (Matthew 28.18–20).

In Matthew the choice of the Twelve is linked with Jesus' compassion for the needs of the crowds. As a human being, with the limitations that brought, Jesus was unable to cope with the numbers needing help. More labourers were needed to bring in the harvest (Matthew 9.35–38). In this context Jesus chooses the Twelve, gives them authority over evil spirits and to heal, and sends them out to preach the gospel of the Kingdom (Matthew 10.1, 7–8; cf. Mark 6.7–13; Luke 9.1–6). Luke tells of another mission of seventy disciples, who seem to have been given similar authority (Luke 10.1, 17–20). Before his ascension Jesus once again commissions the Twelve (though without explicitly mentioning healing), but this time their mission is not to be limited to Israel but is to extend to all nations (Matthew 28.16–20).

At this point it is worth noting that nowhere are the disciples as a group equated with the Kingdom. They form the visible community of the Kingdom, but the parables of the wheat and the tares and of the net show that this is a mixed community. The fact that Jesus delegates to this community the powers of the Kingdom, especially 'the keys of the kingdom' (Matthew 16.17–20; 18.18–20; cf. John 20.23) has sometimes been taken as a basis for equating the Church with the Kingdom. However, that this does not follow seems indicated by the probable background to the 'keys' imagery in Isaiah 22.22, which refers to the king's steward in Judah. The Church is God's agent as he exerts his rule, but not the sole and total embodiment of it.

The Implications for Today

When we turn from considering Jesus' ministry to deciding on its implications for us today, tensions begin to arise between Christians. Here we will present some different perspectives, leaving the reader to decide which are more persuasive.

The Great Commission

The first question we have to ask is whether we should expect Jesus' healing ministry to continue among his followers after his ascension. This is a particularly pertinent question since healing is not explicitly mentioned in any accounts of the post-resurrection commissionings of the apostles by Jesus, apart from the disputed ending of the Gospel of Mark.

It is generally agreed among scholars that Mark 16.9–20 is not original to the Gospel. This agreement rests on the evidence of the earliest manuscripts of the Gospel and the style and vocabulary of these verses when compared with the rest of Mark. This leaves some room for dispute about the status of these verses as part of the canon of authoritative Scripture. Given this uncertainty we would agree with Dr Alan Cole that 'it would be unwise to build any theological position upon these verses alone; and this no responsible Christian group has done', and also heed his later comment, 'Whether or not such evidential manifestations were intended to be continuous in the life of the Church, or restricted to this period, or sporadic, must be considered in the light of the rest of the New Testament; in view of the uncertain textual evidence for this longer Conclusion, no dogmatic assumptions should be made from it alone'.[3] Even here the commission is not 'to preach and to heal' as though they were to be equal parts of their task. Rather, they were commissioned to preach, with the promise that signs would accompany their preaching.

Although it is a promise and not strictly a commissioning, we must take note of John 14.12: '. . . he who believes in me will also do the works that I do; and greater works than these he will do, because I go to the Father'. There is debate about what is meant by 'greater works than these'. Some take it to refer to miraculous deeds. They then usually take the 'greater' to mean 'more numerically' rather than greater in quality, since it is hard to conceive what greater miracles there could be than some of those done by Jesus. However, the context in John's Gospel suggests that the reference is not to miracles. The same phrase 'greater works' has been used by Jesus earlier, in John 5.20–21. Here it refers to the Son giving new life, eternal life, to people.

This leads others to suggest that the 'greater works' refers to the conversions that will come about through the preaching of the gospel by Jesus' followers. This may also be indicated by what Jesus says in John 15.16, 'You did not choose me but I chose you. And I appointed you to go and bear fruit, fruit that will last.' Here the use of the terms 'chosen', 'appointed' and 'go' suggest that what is in Jesus' mind is the apostolic mission to the world, which will be a continuation of his mission to call people to repentance and acceptance of the forgiveness of sins (cf. John 20.21–23). In this case the continuing 'fruit' which Jesus wants his disciples to bear is people who have repented and received forgiveness.

John 10.37–38 is sometimes appealed to as providing some support for understanding the 'works' in John 14.12 as miracles, including miraculous healings. No doubt the works Jesus refers to here do include his miracles. However, it seems probable that what he is stressing here is not their miraculous character alone. Some who witnessed the healing of a man who had been blind from birth were not convinced by this that he came from God (John 9.24, 29; 10.19–21). What Jesus stresses is that the works are 'the works of my Father'. What he means by this is indicated by his discourse in John 8 where he speaks of himself as the Son of the Father in contrast to his opponents who, despite their claim to be sons of Abraham, prove themselves to be sons of the devil because of their desire to kill him and their readiness to reject the truth in favour of lies. In other words, the key test is not the miraculous nature of the works (the devil can work miracles) but their moral and spiritual character.

We must now turn to the 'Great Commission' in Matthew 28.18–20, because different understandings of it lead to different evaluations of what should be the nature of the Church's ministry today, as we shall see.

Neither here nor in the nearest parallels in Luke 24.46–69 and Acts 1.8 is there any explicit command to heal people. How significant is this? Some find it very significant. They point out that the stress here is on the authority of *Jesus*, not on any authority the Eleven may or may not have had to heal and exorcize demons and that there is no earlier command to heal given during Jesus' earthly ministry that can be subsumed under the phrase 'observe all that I have commanded you' here. Hence the Commission is at best silent about any continuing healing ministry. Its clear emphasis is on making disciples who obey Jesus' commands.

Certainly the onus of proof lies on those who argue that a continuing healing ministry is implied here. To begin with they see such an implication in the reference to Jesus' authority. Presumably, they argue, the reason it is mentioned is to encourage Jesus' followers, and it can only be an encouragement if that authority is somehow available to them when they need it. How is it made available?

- One answer may be seen in the promises in Luke 24.49 and Acts 1.8 to the power given to Christians through the gift of the Holy Spirit, and it was by this same power that Jesus cast out demons (Matthew 12.28).
- Another answer is to be seen in the way the early Christians used the name of Jesus in healings and exorcisms (for example, Acts 3.6, 16). Acts 19.13–16 makes clear that this is not simply a matter of using a magic formula. Jesus' name is not to be invoked lightly, but only when one is sure that he will 'own' the use and so invest it with his authority.

Whatever one feels about the persuasiveness of this line of argument, there remains the question whether or not there is a prior command to heal which can be taken as subsumed in the Great Commission. In order to deal with this we must consider the significance of the missions of the Twelve and the Seventy during Jesus' earthly ministry.

The Sending of the Twelve and the Seventy

As we have seen, Jesus gave the Twelve authority to cast out demons and heal. This is reported in all three Synoptic Gospels (Matthew 10.1; Mark 6.7; Luke 9.1). They were instructed at that time to go to the 'lost sheep of the house of Israel' and not to visit the Gentiles. They were sent to preach the message, heal the sick and also raise the dead (Matthew 10.5–7). Mark and Luke record that they reported back after this mission (Mark 6.30; Luke 9.10).

Some Christians regard this as a specific and limited mission of the Twelve which cannot be taken as a pattern for the Church's mission today. Others, however, argue that the authority given to the Twelve here was not intended to be limited to just that particular preaching mission. Indeed, there are several considerations which count against this.

- Matthew does not record any debriefing which might mark the end of their commissioning.
- The reaction of the disciples after their failure with the 'epileptic' boy indicates that they expected to be able to exorcize and heal people. Jesus' reply does not suggest that their expectation is wrong, only that they went about it the wrong way (Matthew 17.20–21; Mark 9.29–30).
- These seem to have been 'training exercises' to prepare them for their future ministry after Jesus' ascension (note how Matthew 10.17ff. is repeated in Mark 13.9ff.). The fact that they are recorded in some detail might indicate that they were understood to provide the pattern for later Christian mission.
- The fact is that in Acts we do find accounts of healings and exorcisms. It is explicitly stated that 'many wonders and miraculous signs were done by the apostles' (2.43), while Paul regarded such things as the hallmarks of being an apostle (2 Corinthians 12.12).

Luke alone also records a separate commissioning of 'seventy others', who were also instructed to heal the sick (Luke 10.1–20). Some regard this as a widening of the earlier mission given to the Twelve. However, others argue that this venture is more strictly circumscribed. They were sent out as an advance party to every place on Jesus' immediate itinerary. Furthermore, their return and debriefing was duly recorded, so making this a separate, self-contained event unrelated to the sending out of the Twelve. It is therefore argued that neither the sending out of the twelve apostles nor the sending of the seventy others can be safely taken to apply more generally in space and time, especially to the Great Commission to 'go and make disciples of all nations . . . to the very end of the age' (Matthew 28.19–20).

So, were these simply one-off events concerning the breaking in of the Kingdom of God and the unique authority of Jesus and his apostles from which we cannot generalize, or were they training missions preparing the disciples and setting the pattern for Christian mission after the ascension? If they were one-off events they cannot safely be taken to apply more generally, or be taken to be assumed as relevant background to the Great Commission and a guide to understanding what is meant when Jesus says in it that the Eleven are to teach their converts to 'observe all that I have commanded you'.

However, even if the missions of the Twelve and the Seventy were not just one-off events we still have to face the question whether the authority referred to in Matthew 28.18 was limited just to the ministry of the apostles.

Healing in the New Testament Church

Luke tells us that authority similar to that given to the Twelve was given to the seventy (compare Luke 9.1 with Luke 10.17–20) and in the book of Acts miracles, including healings and exorcisms, are done by people other than the Twelve, e.g. Stephen (Acts 6.8) and Philip (Acts 8.5–7), not to mention Paul. The fact that the commission in Matthew 28.18–20 (whatever it involves) is given 'until the end of the age' also means that it extends beyond the apostolic era.

Even if Mark 16.9–20 is not canonical, it does witness to belief in the early church that there was an ongoing ministry of healing and exorcism. It has been suggested that these verses were originally a first-century catechismal summary of the post-resurrection appearances of Jesus, which was appended to Mark. Certainly virtually all that is in these verses can be found in the other Gospels and Acts. This has been used as a basis for arguing that the promises given there were fulfilled in the apostolic era and so have no further validity. However, the open-endedness of the promise to 'those who believe' is a basis for arguing against this. It is worth noting that the incident of Paul and the viper in Acts 28.3–6 indicates how we should understand Mark 16.18, which has been subject to strange interpretations. It is a promise of protection against danger, not an invitation to foolhardy risk-taking.

The apostle Paul expected an ongoing ministry of healings to exist within the Church (1 Corinthians 12.28). In fact he refers to gifts (plural) of healings and distinguishes these from 'the working of miracles', so quite what specific gifts he has in mind is unclear. It is true that other lists of gifts in the New Testament (Romans 12.4ff.; Ephesians 4.7ff.; 1 Peter 4.10ff.) do not mention healing, but then no list is exhaustive and the content of each seems determined by the context. The gift of evangelist is mentioned only once (Ephesians 4.11), but that does not mean that it was a gift for a temporary period only, or that it is of minor importance.

James 5.14–15 also speaks of prayer for healing in the Church, though this seems limited to those who are Christians, or at least adherents of the Church.

Theological Arguments

There are two theological grounds for arguing that the Church has a continuing ministry of healings. These are based on what has been said about the significance of healing in Jesus' ministry.

We have seen that the healings were part of what was expected to happen when God's kingly rule broke into this world. This is because disease of all kinds is the antithesis of the wholeness of the person which God's *shalom* brings. Since the Church is the agent of the kingdom and continues Jesus' mission of preaching the gospel of the Kingdom, it is natural that it should include in this a healing ministry. Jesus' healings and exorcisms were part of the 'clash of kingdoms' which resulted as he freed people from Satan's rule. Satan is a defeated enemy, but has not been destroyed (Ephesians 6.10–12; 1 Peter 5.8). Christians have the authority given by Christ to oppose Satan, and this might be expected to be expressed sometimes in healings.

The motive of compassion which characterized Jesus' healing ministry is something that applies as much to Christians today and is another reason why the Church must have a continuing healing ministry. Historically, of course, this has been an important reason why Christians have played a major role in the development of health care worldwide.

Why Are Miracles So Rare?

To say, on theological grounds, that the Church should have a continuing healing ministry, leaves open the question of the nature and form of that ministry. We are back to the question, should it expect to replicate Jesus' ministry? Should it expect to perform the kind of healings which he did by similar means? If it should, we have to admit that something went wrong, because for most of Church history it has not done so.

Lack of Faith

For some people the answer is simple, it is the result of a lack of faith. In order to evaluate this possibility we must give some more consideration to the relationship between faith and healing in Jesus' ministry.

There is one incident in Jesus' ministry when a failure to heal (actually, exorcize) is linked with a lack of faith in those attempting to bring about the healing. That is the case of the 'epileptic' boy (Matthew 17.14–20; Mark 9.14–29; Luke 9.37–42). Jesus' reply to the disciples' question, 'Why could we not cast it out' is different in Mark and Matthew. In Mark it is, 'This kind cannot be driven out by anything but prayer' (the balance of evidence indicates that the additional words 'and fasting' which are found in some manuscripts were not in the text originally, but were added later by someone while copying the text). There is no reference to faith here, but Jesus' initial reaction to the situation, 'O faithless generation', indicates that he did see a failure of faith here. Matthew makes this explicit by reporting the answer as, 'Because of your little faith'. He then adds a saying about faith which Luke includes in a quite different context (Luke 17.6). It seems that Matthew is giving an interpretation of the somewhat enigmatic reply reported in Mark, using another of Jesus' sayings.

Two important points seem to come out of this incident. The first is that very little faith is needed to produce great effects. This is the point of the saying which Matthew adds to the story. Only a mustard seed ('the smallest of all the seeds', Mark 4.31) quantity is needed! The same point is implied in the longer Marcan form of the story, in which Jesus responds to the father's wavering half-belief, 'I believe; help my unbelief'. Here there is no encouragement for the idea that one needs to 'work up' a large quantity of faith in order to be healed or to be able to heal. The second point is the implicit linking of faith and prayer in the story in Mark, a link which Matthew saw since he interpreted Jesus' saying about prayer as being one about faith. This same link is found in the Marcan form of the saying in Matthew 17.20 (Mark 11.22–25). What is the link? Surely it is that true prayer means an openness to, and dependence upon, God. As such it is an expression of faith in God, trusting the situation to him and being willing to accept his way of dealing with it. Perhaps the disciples' problem was not that they did not believe that they, or God, could heal the boy. They seemed genuinely surprised that they had not succeeded. Perhaps their problem was that they were so confident of their ability to cope with the situation that they did not pray, seeking God's way of dealing with it. Faith is not a commodity which we use in order to purchase results. It is an openness to receive what God will give.

This understanding of faith makes sense of the inability of Jesus to heal more than a few people on his visit to Nazareth. The problem this time did not lie in the healer, Jesus, but in the fact that the populace in general were not prepared to receive healing from him. It hurt their pride too much!

A twofold conclusion might be drawn from this (a third possibility is discussed later under 'What Is God Doing Today?').

- First, we have to take seriously the possibility that, like the disciples in this incident, we are wrongly closed (for whatever reasons) to what God wants to do through the Church in terms of a healing ministry, and that this is why we have seen little of the kind of healings Jesus did.
- However, second, it is also possible that in western, secular society, we are in a situation akin to that which Jesus faced in Nazareth. The attitude of the society towards receiving healing through prayer is such that God can do little for them by this means.

It is not easy to see how one can weigh the relative importance of these two factors. The responsibility of Christians must surely be to try to ensure that we are as open as possible to God working through us in whatever ways he desires.

Spiritual Opposition

Having raised the issue of the relevance of the spiritual state of a society to the effectiveness of a healing ministry, it is worth pursuing this a bit further. It has become fairly commonplace for missiologists to take up the image of a 'clash of kingdoms' when speaking of the impact of the gospel on a non-Christian culture. Within this context they stress the significance of 'power encounters' as events which serve to vindicate the truth of the message and encourage people to accept it. They see that they need not fear the power of their former god(s) because of the superior power of the Christian God. In the ministry of Jesus it was healings and exorcisms that provided the power encounters. The same is said to be true in some modern missionary situations. Whether such Christ-like healings actually occur is open to dispute. Medical details in these situations can be very difficult to verify. Attempts that have been made to substantiate these claims have run into great difficulties, as they do in western societies. But even if such things are happening on missionary frontiers should we expect this in all situations, and particularly in western secular societies?

Even in Jesus' ministry by no means all who witnessed amazing healings responded by repentance and faith. Those who do not want to believe will always find ways around the evidence (e.g. by attributing Jesus' power to Satan). It is possible that in a secular society which is highly sceptical of anything 'spiritual' the impact of healing miracles will be even less. They may even be counter-productive in that some may be frightened by them, fearing the unknown, and so avoid those who claim to perform them, while others will simply reject them as too weird to be true. In such a situation effective 'power encounters' (in terms of leading to belief in Jesus) will take a different form. They might, for example, take place in the moral, rather than physical, realm – remarkable change in attitudes and values which leads to someone being as much a 'new person' as a healed paralytic. After all, Satan can 'bind' people so that they are moral cripples. This is not to say that healing miracles can have no place in a western secular, rationalistic society, only that it may not be surprising that they have had a much smaller place than in some other societies. It may be that with the increase in various forms of spirituality and occultism in the west, and the consequent greater openness to spiritual realities and powers, the balance is set to change.

Talk of 'power encounters' can be dangerous in that it could obscure the fact that it is the gospel which is 'the power of God for salvation to everyone who has faith' (Romans 1.16). We must remember that 'signs and wonders' of all forms are not to be regarded as ends in themselves, but as supports for the preaching of the gospel. In the New Testament they are not a substitute for preaching the gospel, but an accompaniment to it. In fact there is a sense in which, in Jesus' ministry, healing and exorcism take a second place to preaching. This is indicated in Mark 1.38, where Jesus turns his back on many needy sick people to go and preach in places where the gospel of the Kingdom has not yet been heard. Of course he healed people and cast out demons in these places too, but his emphasis seems to have been on proclaiming the gospel, with healings as an accompaniment, rather than on the healings themselves. His hesitancy about healing the Syro-Phoenician woman's daughter is probably best seen in this way too. Jesus did not want to be drawn into an indiscriminate healing ministry because he still had a commitment to preaching to the Jews first to be fulfilled. It is clear that for Jesus the healing flowed from, and supported, the preaching. He did not allow it to control or replace it. This does not contradict what we have said about his motivation of compassion for the physically needy.

It is in fact the result of a deeper compassion. Healed bodies will still be subject to disease, pain, death and dissolution. However, people have eternal destinies. It is therefore more important that their spiritual need is met. This, of course, should not be wrongly polarized into an either/or situation. But it does mean that we need to recognize that there is a priority about the call to repent and believe in the gospel.

What Is God Doing Today?

A quite different approach to the rarity (or absence) of healing miracles today is possible. This is to say that, in his sovereign purposes, God just is not working in that way today. Rather, he works through the framework of the world which he has created. Within this framework there are inbuilt healing processes and people gifted with healing skills. This is quite different from saying that he has not worked through miracles in the past (in Jesus' ministry, for example) or that he cannot. It is rather to say that, given the uncertainty in drawing implications from the biblical material, we must take seriously the evidence of what is actually happening as an indication of how God is choosing to work. God reveals his purposes in his works as well as his words. Scholars sometimes talk of the 'two books' of God's revelation – the 'book of nature' and the 'book of Scripture'. In nature God reveals something of himself in what he has created. In the Bible we have a fuller revelation, centred on his work of redemption. The evidence of the two 'books' must be held together because the same God lies behind both, as Creator and Redeemer. So, it is argued, since we see few, *if any*, miraculous healings of the kind Jesus performed happening today, despite the fact that many Christians do pray for healing, we must take this seriously as evidence that God is not working in that way now. Moreover, the evidence of Church history suggests that this has been the case for a long time past.

Wide enquiries have been made over a considerable period of time without finding convincing evidence that healing miracles of the kind done by Jesus are occurring today in the UK.[4] It has not been easy to assess evidence from other countries, but where careful examination has been possible it has not been any more convincing than that from the UK. By 'the kind done by Jesus' is meant the instantaneous, complete healing of incurable physical diseases, at a word of command, without other therapy and in conditions with no known incidence of spontaneous remission. This is not to say that all Jesus' healings fell within this tight definition, but most did and any ministry that claims to be a continuation of Jesus' should, arguably, include such miracles. Only three cases of miracle have been claimed officially at Lourdes within the past twenty-five years and they have all been open to dispute. One involved a spontaneous remission of a cancer that took place gradually over an extended period, leaving a displaced hip joint. Another lacked clear evidence of neurological damage before the healing or coherent explanation of the man's symptoms. He may have been an hysteric. The third did not happen instantaneously and depended on a particular interpretation of the nature of a bone tumour.

A story that was written up in a book[5] and later presented on television[6] highlights the sort of complexities and misunderstanding that can occur. A newborn baby had a tumour of the arm. A National Health Consultant said that the tumour was malignant and had been miraculously healed.

It turned out that the doctor who presented the case had not actually been involved in the care of this child nor in the medical decisions that were made. The first question that had to be addressed was whether or not the tumour really was malignant. Although these particular tumours are rare, it seems that 90 per cent of them do not spread to distant parts of the body, which is what the word 'malignant' usually implies. The surgeon was reluctant to perform mutilating surgery if it could possibly be avoided, as he could see no surgical alternative to amputating the arm. The cancer specialist thought the tumour would respond to chemotherapy, but such high doses of drugs would be needed that they would have very serious effects on such a small baby.

As it was a rare tumour, they took advice from other specialists. They were given good reason to believe that this type of tumour could well resolve spontaneously if left alone. Soft tissue tumours in the newborn commonly do.[7] As it was unlikely to spread to other parts of the body, the doctors in charge of the case decided to keep the child under review, holding their therapeutic options in reserve. As they hoped, over the next six months the tumour gradually disappeared. The case was sufficiently unusual to justify writing it up in a medical journal.[8] The surgeon and cancer specialist were both indignant that the recovery had been presented as being miraculous. There was certainly nothing instantaneous about it, and the disease followed the course they had been led to expect.

Of course medical details in these matters are not easy for lay people to understand. Medical training would not continue for so many years if the subject matter was simple. The lay perception of a situation may well differ from an informed medical one. The fact that a doctor gives a case a name may seem to imply a sure diagnosis of a physical condition. Doctors know that is not always the case. A variety of factors can lead the best doctor to a faulty diagnosis, and only the future development of the condition, maybe recovery from it, can confirm or falsify the diagnosis. To speak of 'spontaneous remission' may sound like special pleading of the worse kind, but doctors know that it does occur and is a feature of many conditions. The relationship between body and mind is intimate. It can affect the symptoms of certain diseases in subtle ways. Because doctors are well aware of these kinds of considerations many are more cautious than lay people in accepting claims of miraculous healing.

To attribute the lack of miraculous healings to scepticism in our society may be misguided, since there seems to be a readiness to believe in all sorts of 'miracles' – from spoon-bending to psychic surgery. Among Christians there have, over the last twenty-five years, been large numbers in the west who have confidently expected miracles, yet the ones they claim have occurred do not stand up to rigorous examination. The fact that some conditions are healed while others are not could well have more to do with the disease process than either the faith of the patient on the one hand or the mysterious sovereign purposes of God on the other. Motor neurone disease never recovers. Some cancers occasionally do. AIDS is never cured. Chronic Fatigue (so-called 'ME') usually does go away. A child who is developmentally delayed may surprise everyone. A Down's Syndrome child will retain the same genetic configuration in each cell of the body throughout life. The question of the sovereign purpose of God is then pushed back to the question why he allows certain individuals to suffer from particular conditions, rather than why he allows some to recover.

Conclusions

Despite our differences in outlook Christians can agree on some conclusions.

We can accept that prayer for healing has a valid, indeed important, place in Christian experience and ministry. Some remarkable recoveries do occur in answer to prayer, when humanly speaking no hope remains. Explanations for this may differ but are of secondary importance, provided unjustifiable claims are not made on an uninformed basis. These are dishonouring to God and can be pastorally harmful. The great pastoral question in any given situation is, 'How should we pray?'. It is natural to desire the well-being of loved ones, and it is right to express this to God in prayer for healing. However, as in all our prayers our ultimate concern must be to discern God's will for a particular situation, and so it is not a lack of faith to pray, 'Thy will be done'. In some cases it may be that, like Paul, the person who is seeking healing has to learn to live with the condition in the strength given by God's grace (2 Corinthians 12.7–12). In others there may be complete recovery. The big question is whether, and how, we can discern God's detailed will in a given case. Part of the relevant information is what is known about the disease and what it implies. Until the Kingdom of God comes in its fullness we must take seriously the truth that we live in perishable bodies which are wasting away (see 1 Corinthians 15.42 and 2 Corinthians 4.16). We must put this information alongside any sense of discernment of God's will that comes to us as we pray about the situation. Of course it is wise for a person close to someone needing healing, and so emotionally involved in the situation, to pray together with other, less emotionally involved, people because this lessens the danger of confusing our desires with God's will.

One area of difference between Christians with regard to prayer for healing is over the level of expectation with regard to the result. Some do believe that healings like those Jesus performed should happen today fairly often, others do not. However, there is probably wide agreement that we should avoid two extremes. It is wrong to deny that prayer has any value. God has a habit of surprising his people. He can, and from time to time does, far more than we ask or think (Ephesians 3.20). It is equally wrong, as we have seen, to treat prayer as magic formula that will guarantee results, or to view faith as a commodity we can offer to God and in response to which he has to do what we ask. Furthermore we would do well to use the word 'miracle' sparingly and not devalue it. Something that is a fairly common occurrence is not a miracle! It ceases to be a cause of wonder, to use the biblical terminology.

Another area of agreement is that, since at any time very many people are unwilling, for whatever reason, to turn to Jesus directly for healing of the kind recorded in the Gospels, it is natural that Christian compassion, no doubt led by the Holy Spirit, has resulted in the development of healing through medicine and surgery. This is not to be seen as an inferior kind of ministry, a second-best substitute for healing through 'spiritual' means alone. It is a genuine expression of Jesus' compassion for the needy. As such it can be a 'sign' which supports the gospel and opens some to its message as they see the love of God demonstrated in the care given by the nurse and doctor. We must not drive a wedge between different modes of God's healing care for people or we will end up divorcing the Creator from the Saviour. This means that in practice we should strive for a cooperation in healing administered through medicine and surgery and healing administered through prayer. Whether or not it has failed in terms of a 'miraculous' healing ministry, it is clear that the Church in the west has failed seriously by letting medicine and surgery come to be seen as standing over against 'spiritual healing' rather than as also being the work of God.

We can also agree that, like Jesus, the Church has the primary mission of preaching the gospel of the Kingdom, and its healing ministry flows from and supports this. It is not an end in itself.

References

1. C.E.B. Cranfield, *The Gospel According to St Mark* (Cambridge University Press 1972), pp. 251–252.
2. For example: Psalm 106.4–5; Hosea 9.9; the verb used here has the connotation of carrying out an inspection.
3. A. Cole, *Mark: An Introduction and Commentary* (Tyndale Press 1961), pp. 259, 262.
4. V. Edmunds and G.C. Scorer, *Some Thoughts on Faith Healing* (Christian Medical Fellowship 1979), third edition; P.G. May, *Looking for a Miracle* (Harper Collins 1995).
5. D. Lewis *Healing: Fiction, Fantasy or Fact?* (Hodder & Stoughton 1.989), pp. 221–228.
6. *Heart of the Matter*, Roger Bolton Productions. Shown on BBC 1, 16 August 1992.
7. *British Journal of Cancer* 66 (1992), Suppl. XVIII, S80–83.
8. *British Journal of Cancer* 66 (1992), Suppl. XVIII, S72–75.

CHAPTER 5

Suffering

Revd Dr Nigel Wright
Mrs Sheila Smith

The healing ministry of the Church is part of its practical response to the existence of suffering in the world. Accounting for the existence of suffering is a challenge that faces all the world's religions. The problem of suffering is grappled with in various ways in the Hebrew Scriptures, most notably in the books of Psalms and Job. The early Christians found that the sufferings of Jesus and his resurrection from the dead brought a new dimension to their grapplings with the problem. In this chapter an experienced counsellor dialogues with a theologian about the mainlines of Christian thinking on the problem of suffering and how this relates to the practical work of pastoral care of those who are actually suffering.

A Panorama of Suffering

Even a fairly cursory glance at volumes such as the Oxford English Dictionary, Chambers Twentieth Century English Dictionary or Roget's Thesaurus makes it clear that suffering is something that occurs in many different areas of human experience. It is closely connected with the occurrence of pain. Pain, of course, can be primarily physical, mental, emotional or spiritual in origin, but in any one instance there is probably a mixture of all these aspects. We can even experience it as a result of sharing someone else's suffering, either by empathizing with them or by actually sharing their situation with them.

Before discussing suffering as both a theological and pastoral challenge it is worth recognizing the wide spectrum of human situations in which it arises. Below is a list of some specific examples of situations which inevitably result in suffering in one form or another, and sometimes in a number of different ways.

- Disease or sickness of all kinds, but especially long-term, incurable and painful conditions such as: cancer, AIDS, diabetes and heart conditions.
- Mental illness in various forms. This may be related to various kinds of emotional and spiritual distress.
- Natural disasters such as drought, earthquakes, tempests, which leave death and destruction in their wake.
- The consequences of war: injury, death, grief, hostage-taking, torture – the list could be greatly expanded.
- Being persecuted, tortured, even martyred, for being different from the majority community in some way, whether it be in race, religion or ideology.
- Breakdown in relationships of various kinds: family, marital, church, work and internationally.
- The consequences of dependency, such as on drugs and alcohol, including the personal, health and financial consequences for the abuser and society.
- The consequences of one person abusing another: child abuse, sexual abuse, more general violence and emotional blackmail.
- Loss, separation or deprivation, especially that associated with the death of loved ones.
- Facing one's own death and dying, or sharing that similar journey with others.

To these general experiences of humankind we might add yet another aspect of suffering, namely, there is that which we suffer because we choose to follow Christ. Christ suffered, both because he shared the sufferings of others and because he was obedient to the call of his Father God. Therefore, as God's people we also may suffer because we have compassion and because we receive the ridicule and misunderstanding which can be meted out to those who seek to follow Jesus. It is in the command to us to declare the Kingdom of God and to be involved in enabling its coming, that Jesus warns us that if we follow him we take up our cross daily.

It is an interesting fact that Jesus, in calling us to be involved in the coming of his Kingdom, used this 'taking up of our cross' in the context of being *at work*, rather than in terms of being sick and unable to work. This of course does not mean that sickness is not an experience of suffering but it is simply a matter of where the emphasis actually comes. It is common for Christians to use the word 'suffering' in equation with sickness. This understanding can diminish that larger panorama of recognizing many, many other situations where deep suffering occurs.

It is certain that the readers will be able to add many more examples to this list, from their own life experience and from sharing the experiences of others. The point is that suffering is indeed a panorama. It is not something which is readily or easily defined. Indeed, it is unwise pastorally to limit an understanding and recognition of suffering simply from our own knowledge and experience. There is a sense in which suffering is 'in the eye of the beholder'. What may be experienced as suffering by one person is not necessarily the same for another and vice versa. Moreover, it needs to be remembered that all we experience as human beings, reaches us at more than a physical level. Even if the physical aspect is the primary source, suffering reaches us also in the mind and mental areas, as well as in the emotional, social and spiritual aspects of our total being. It is unpredictable as to where the emphasis may occur, or where it may change in the course of an experience of suffering. The pastoral challenge therefore, is to listen and to understand where individuals find themselves, at any given time within their journey of suffering.

Suffering is part of the common lot of humanity in its experience of the assaults of evil. In the face of this people often need help in disentangling their experience and their faith. Christians need help in interpreting their responsibility to imitate Christ, both in the alleviation of, and the overcoming of, suffering. While some of God's people may be called to have a particular service in pastoral care or in the political or social concern, none of us is exempt from Christ's command to love one another, especially in sharing the burdens due to suffering.

The Theological Problem of Suffering

The panorama of suffering that we have surveyed helps to explain the fact that the problem of suffering has been an intractable and perennial subject for Christian reflection. Of course it becomes most acute when we are faced with actual instances of vicious and apparently meaningless pain inflicted by humans upon each other or simply by inexplicable fate. This chapter does not pretend that it is offering an 'answer' but assumes the position that suffering is the open wound with which we have to learn to live. There are, however, ways of living with the problem that have both intellectual and personal integrity.

Christian responses to the problem of suffering tend to fall into two categories which we may broadly distinguish as the philosophical and the mystical.

The Philosophical Response

This attempts to answer at a theoretical level the classic objection of David Hume: 'Is (God) willing to prevent evil, but not able? Then he is impotent. Is he able, but not willing? Then he is malevolent. Is he both able and willing? Whence then is evil?'.

The resolution of this objection has been found traditionally in the so-called 'free-will defence', the argument that authentic creaturely freedom requires the possibility of evil and is the ground of its actuality. So, it can be argued that God's omnipotence does not include the power to do that which is logically impossible, the creation, for instance, of a square circle. To create free creatures who are incapable of misusing their freedom is logically impossible. Yet love requires the creation of such free creatures. So the omnipotence and love of God can be reconciled with the creation of a world in which evil is possible and, indeed, actual because of the actions of free creatures.

The Mystical Response

On the philosophical level the free-will defence is both strong and coherent. It is not easily refuted. The second category of response however, which we are calling the 'mystical', is inclined to find it inadequate on the ground that it does not reach people who are actually suffering. Arguments about God and suffering, from this perspective are not so much to do with philosophy as with protest; protest against the pain that creatures must endure. The question to be answered is not the cool and detached 'Why does God allow creatures to suffer?' so much as the red-hot and passionate 'Where is God when creatures suffer?'.

Here, the resources of the Christian faith are drawn out in a particular way by reflection upon the cross. God is the crucified

God, the one who has endured physical and psychological pain to the ultimate degree, who has tasted death for the sake of all. The cross of Christ is an event in the very heart of God, a trinitarian reality whereby the Son embraces dying and death as, with and for creation, and the Father endures in grief the loss of his own Son. Furthermore, in the cross we see that God takes up into himself the whole history of human suffering.

Wherever there is pain in creaturely experience, such pain is endured also by the God in whom we live and who in compassion sympathizes with us. God is to be found most especially, therefore, in the sufferings of the suffering. As the resurrection speaks of God's own triumph over death in Christ so it also gives hope to creatures that their own sufferings will be transfigured into blessedness by the participation of God in our own existence. This remains a future hope of sharing the blessedness of God, but may be known in a measure even in present sufferings through the presence of God which counts for far more than philosophical speculation. Indeed, there is virtue to be found in living without philosophical answers. It is in the acceptance of the mysteries and the unresolved tensions of life, the dark side of our pilgrimage, that the growth of authentic personhood becomes possible. Yet suffering is not to be passively endured or accepted with resignation. In compassionate struggle against suffering, especially that of others, we prove our courage and our capacity to resemble God in his compassion for us. We know we cannot protect others from suffering, but by our compassionate presence and aid we can help them to pass through it. All depends, therefore, on how we respond with God's help to our fate and the degree to which we convert our suffering into positive growth.

Even here there is recognition that such a conversion may need to await the transformation of all things in the fullness of time. No guarantee is given that 'answers' will be forthcoming in the present age, only that God's ultimate answer is awaited and may, from time to time, be prefigured and anticipated in our experience as it has been prefigured in the resurrection of Christ. To the philosophical response to suffering there is added in this way a mystical response, either as an alternative to replace it or as a complement to it on the pastoral level.

The extent to which the mystical response can be held on to may be dependent on the degree of suffering we are called to undergo or to witness. At the end of the day the real problem consists not in the fact that there should be *some* suffering but in the overwhelming quantity of it. There are times when what confronts us is so destructive, malicious and cruel that no response other than that of total rejection appears adequate and all hope of transfiguration vanishes. It is hard not to feel the moral weight of those who in all honesty come to this position. Easy judgements and condemnations are not possible. Belief in the goodness of God may need to be maintained in the face of strong evidence to the contrary. The wise believer strengthens him- or herself, by acute empathy with others, to face such a trial of faith in the midst of life.

Interlude

We have attempted to sketch the theological landscape and something of the pastoral demand which lie before us. Before we go on to develop some tentative reflections which may help to integrate more effectively the theological and pastoral dimensions of the matter, it will be helpful to consider two traditions of response to the fact of suffering which run through the history of Christian thought about the subject. These are sometimes called the 'Augustinian' and the 'Irenaean' responses. The former tends to see suffering as a direct consequence of human sin. The latter tradition suggests that at least some suffering may instead be a consequence of finitude, part of a 'soul-making' experience that belongs to earthly pilgrimage.

THE AUGUSTINIAN TRADITION

The 'free-will defence' has focused for its cogency upon the persistent human unwillingness to live in harmony with the will of God. The negative phenomena of human and creaturely existence have been understood as the consequence of human sin. For much of the Church's history it was possible to argue that God created a good and perfect world. The present imperfections were the direct consequence of Adam's sin through which the courses of humanity and of nature were diverted from their original perfection. The motif of fall and redemption was therefore a key signature and the story of a Paradise Lost a basic paradigm of Christian understanding. With the scientific revolution it became increasingly difficult to hold this position in an unreconstructed form. The fossil records revealed that dying, death and pain had been present in the animal creation prior to the emergence of humanity. The theory of evolution posited that the emergence and development of natural life was actually by the very means of struggle and conflict. The capacity for pain and actual suffering were, apparently, part of the very fabric of created existence.

This elementary fact, revealed at so many levels by so many sciences, could not but affect Christian interpretation of reality. Various responses are, of course, possible. Some have chosen the pathway of denial, arguing that scientific accounts of origins are badly flawed. 'Creation scientists' argue for an extensive reinterpretation of contemporary sciences on what is supposedly a biblical basis. The Bible is taken as giving literal science and comprehensive theories are elaborated to show how scientific knowledge (as opposed to what is argued to be pseudo-scientific theory) can be squared with the literal narrative of Scripture. These approaches serve to remind us that scientific theories must always remain provisional. Yet large questions are left about how both scientific discoveries and biblical texts are to be properly understood. Few informed observers, from whatever discipline, find the position convincing. Clearly the attempt is being made by this means to preserve the notion that all suffering springs from the misuse of human free-will.

An alternative view acknowledges the fact of pre-human, pre-fall suffering in creation but goes on to find an origin of this in a transcendent sphere. Before the fall of humanity there took place an angelic fall, a cosmic rupture occasioned by the rebellion of Lucifer against the Creator. The pre-human creation is indeed corrupted and distorted but is so by virtue of the rebellion of its angelic guardians who have precipitated creation into its state of conflict 'red in tooth and claw'. The free-will defence is thus preserved in that the misuse of creaturely freedom by angelic beings accounts for suffering in the non-human creation. Human beings in their turn add to this by falling prey to the now-fallen powers and contributing their energies to the chaos.

The notion of a cosmic 'angelic catastrophe' has an ancient pedigree and bears careful reflection. It seeks to be true to the biblical impression that humans came into a world which was already in jeopardy (the tempting serpent in Paradise). It points to the fact that rebellion and resistance against God is on a wider front than the merely human. It introduces us to a wider 'mystery of iniquity' in a way which has echoes in Christian experience down the centuries. Its weakness lies in the lack of clear biblical foundations for its claims, relying as it does on inference from unclear texts, and in the highly mythological language which it is forced to employ. But again, it works within the framework of the free-will defence, only it locates a prior misusable freedom in a transcendent rather than an earthly source.

THE IRENAEAN TRADITION

The category of response we have been examining fits generally into a tradition which takes its inspiration from Augustine. A different, but not entirely dissimilar, tradition is associated with Irenaeus, (although we are not suggesting that these formative thinkers anticipated everything that has been developed from their insights). While the Augustinian model keeps close to the creation-fall-redemption motif, the Irenaean model is to be seen more in what we might call 'evolutionary developmental' terms. According to this view, we are not to think of a human fall from an original perfection. Rather, creation is moving towards fulfilment and perfection without having yet attained it. Humanity is created as a central part of this movement towards the fulfilment of creation but at a distance from it so that they might seek after it. It is with, through and by a humanity in communion with God that the world is decisively drawn towards its consummation. The fall consists in the failure of humanity to continue in the right direction and enable creation to attain its goal. It is a genuine fall in that it is a fall away from the potential of attaining to the consummation and in this sense represents a decay of the original creation. Adam and Eve are not completed creatures who fall away from perfection, but learners and pilgrims created to move towards completion but who fall away from their vocation and destiny and so suppress the development of the wider creation. In that they fall short of their goal, creation itself, intimately bound up with them, must fall short of its goal. Its potential remains unrealized.

This Irenaean tradition would on the face of it appear to be more congruent with what is known of the world from other sources. It allows us to think of a world in process of development and fits in with the divine mandate to humanity to have dominion, to multiply and subdue the earth. God's purposes for them were only at their beginning and yet the primal human decision against God has moved things in the wrong direction. The goodness of the world does not consist, on this understanding, in its being statically already perfected and complete but in its potential for development, its freedom to grow and to become, to realize its inherent potential. The world exists under the command to journey towards its ultimate goal of corresponding to God and his glory. The creation was declared 'very good' (Genesis 1.31) because it suited God's soul-making purpose, not because it was already perfected. It provided a suitable context for human beings to grow and become, to realize in freedom their inherent potential and so suited God's purpose.

So God grants space and time to humanity, nurturing humanity's freedom because his goal is to win from them through grace the free response of love and cooperation. But, and here we make room for suffering, the upward call towards completion implies in the present order of things the possibility and reality of the incomplete and the imperfect. Movement towards a goal which is free and uncompelled holds open the possibility of dead-ends, wrong turns and errors. As the archetype of this freedom, human beings in their wrong turns suppress creation at large and prevent its development towards its goal. Suffering in some dimensions may thus be part of the givenness of finite existence.

Suffering, Cure and Healing

Healing and Cure

What has been said so far in this chapter might seem to put a question mark against talk of healing, in view of what has been said about the inevitability of suffering as a common human experience in life. It seems necessary to point out that 'healing' is not an alternative meaning for 'cure'.

A gastric ulcer can be 'cured' by medication and perhaps where necessary by surgery. But if the underlying cause of the ulcer is psychosomatic (it was emotionally or psychologically triggered), then 'cure' deals only with the effect. Healing of the underlying cause is something both different and more profound. Healing, when linked with the idea of wholeness, means that as human beings, we experience a touch of the love and comfort, the wholesomeness of God, at a level which is deeper and more precious than merely the release of pain. We have been reminded of the work of the cross, when Jesus took upon himself, and suffered for, the pain and sin of the world. Resurrection, which followed crucifixion now gives us hope that while we suffer, there is a comfort in a spiritual sense. This surpasses the pain and the suffering, enabling us to find something, (mysterious though it is), which becomes more valuable than the suffering itself. It changes suffering from something which is meaning*less* to something meaning*ful*. Thus, healing can be seen to be different from cure. Cure is about an *absence* of pain, healing is about something with an eternal *presence*, more valuable than pain.

Is All Suffering Creative?

Having said this, we need to heed Nigel's comment that 'suffering is not to be passively endured or accepted with resignation'. Perhaps this is the point where we might address the issue of what is some-times called the 'permissive' will of God and suffering. Although we may firmly believe that God's love can take and transform suffering into good, there still remains the issue of how we should respond when faced with different forms of suffering. Unjust actions or attitudes engender suffering. Surely, in these cases, our emphasis must be on seeking to deal with the cause, rather than simply saying 'we can trust God to make something good out of it'. Ignorance may be another cause of some suffering. Inappropriate harshness in correcting or training of the young, or in civil or criminal punishment, might come into this category. There would seem to be a number of forms of suffering in which social and/or political action is required to aim at alleviating it, rather than 'blaming' God for allowing the situation. We are called to exercise justice as well as care and compassion.

Suffering and Growth

Nigel also reminds us that if we are to convert our suffering into positive growth we need God's help. We have to trust the work of the Holy Spirit of God to effect this transformation within us. Of ourselves we are not able to do it. It may help our understanding to think in terms of natural 'life'. The seed we put into the ground eventually becomes the fruit. We do not understand how, but it is in fact our faith which leads us to plant it and to hope. So it is, with the 'seeds' of our suffering. Our faith and our hope have to live together, that this transformation through the mysterious work of the Holy Spirit will actually occur. We shall experience the fruit of it within our own being. We might call this God's peace, his 'shalom'. This is the energy and the resource which is given us to go on living. This in turn becomes that real, yet intangible, source of enabling and of hope and comfort that another can receive from us – the fruit of the Spirit – as we share each other's burdens.

Here I would like to share a 'picture' of long-standing comfort and restoration. Two pairs of hands, each pair side-by-side and opened, lie on top of one another. Below, the large, strong pair support the small pair above. The smaller hands hold a package (a 'burden'). The smaller hands are the tangible, seemingly obvious, support, yet in actuality they do not carry anywhere near the full weight, because they are supported by the large, strong hands. He who calls us to love one another and to bear one another's burdens also says, 'Come to me, all you who are weary and burdened, and I will give you rest. Take my yoke upon you and learn from me, for I am gentle and humble in heart, and you will find rest for your souls. For my yoke is easy and my burden is light' (Matthew 11.28–30 NIV). Jesus does not indicate the absence of toil or suffering, but promises that through his presence and his direction of us, the choice of burden that he puts upon us will be bearable. 'He has borne our griefs and carried our sorrows' in their fullest extent (Isaiah 53.4). We share one another's burdens and pain. But the power both of their burdens and our own sufferings cannot over-whelm us, when we allow ourselves to be supported by the hands of the Risen One who was crucified for us. Wounded and yet being both 'healed' and 'healer', through the power of the Spirit of Christ.

The Personhood of the Carer

This brings us to a consideration of the personhood of the one who offers pastoral care to the sufferer.

Theology and Caring

Undoubtedly there is a need for such a person to have a theological understanding and perspective on this matter. Otherwise, the mind is not engaged and not focused in making contact with another person. However, as we have already seen from our brief survey of Christian approaches to the problem, there is no place for dogmatism and for thinking that there is only one view and one theological understanding of this complex issue. Therefore, on the one hand, we need an understanding, a humble confidence, concerning what we are seeking to do and yet, on the other, we need to be open always to learning from other people's perspectives.

Important though our own theological perspective is, it is important to be extremely sensitive and careful as to when and how that particular perspective is shared with the one who suffers. Initially, a relationship must be formed which enables us to share something of our own comfort, (fruit of our suffering) through the message of 'compassion', rather than through the offer of a theological perspective. Although it is generally the case that our mind normally has control over, and influences, our feeling, it is in times of stress and suffering that our feelings may become uppermost. It then requires effort and repeated practice for the mind to be able to regain control over our emotions. There is a place for the mind to be instructed and to engage in this process of overcoming the control of emotions, but this is usually easier after the feelings have sensed the ministry of compassion.

Compassion and Empathy

Valuable and necessary though it is, neither training nor theological understanding, of themselves, will adequately prepare for this task. Over and over again as we read the Gospels, we are told that Jesus 'had compassion'. This is a costly emotion of empathy, not merely sympathy. Sympathy is one's own projected understanding and feeling towards another's suffering. Empathy is getting close enough, and deep enough into, another's circumstances to be able to feel it in their way, to 'stand in their shoes', and to demonstrate effectively that we are so doing. Unless we have compassion as well as skill, we minister merely through our own limited understanding and life experience, which may be far distant from the sufferers 'here and now'.

The Wounded Healer

We have mentioned theology, training and compassion. A concept that is often mentioned nowadays is that of 'the wounded healer'.

This makes the appropriate point that unless we have experience of exposing our own wounds to the forgiveness and healing of the Spirit of Christ, then our ability to lead others to that place is diminished. St Paul, in 2 Corinthians 1.3–4, urges us to receive this 'comfort' in our trouble, that we may in turn have it to offer others in their suffering. The eternal value of this heavenly, spiritual ministry remains alive and is passed on. We communicate with one another, more deeply and in a much larger variety of ways, than through mere words. The real person that I am, deep within myself, is what another 'hears', far more clearly than what I say. Not only our own suffering, but also the genuine empathizing for others, produces the wounds which respond to the balm of the Comforter, the Holy Spirit of God. Jesus was a 'wounded healer' long before his crucifixion. He had his own human experience of suffering, from which he refused to yield to the temptation of escape. Rather, he sought his Father's comfort. These sufferings of his, which we are called to share, are on behalf of others. His compassion and involvement in identifying with others was costly.

Seeds of Hope

Jesus reminds us that he buried his own human and natural desires: 'I tell you the truth, unless a grain of wheat falls into the ground and dies, it remains only a single seed. But if it dies, it produces many seeds' (John 12.24). He experienced the crushing and breaking, the pain of others' suffering, in order to produce the fruit of the Kingdom of God. We now recognize that fruit in his resurrection power. This conquers the power of suffering and evil and prevents it from overwhelming us. This is our 'hope', to which we cling, in 'faith', as suffering is experienced. As we seek his presence, so we find his 'healing', remembering that this is not the same as 'cure'.

Jesus 'listened' with his ears, eyes, mind, feelings and spirit to others' suffering. He 'heard' their words, their body language, their tone of voice and recognized the pain in their eyes. He allowed the Holy Spirit of God to also awaken him to their spiritual state. All this was costly and painful. When we open ourselves to such an awareness of others, we shall suffer. That will lead us back to the Father for comfort and healing, to enable us to continue further, to receive more comfort, to give yet again to others.

Not Overwhelmed

Alongside the above we must take note of John 16.33. Jesus said, 'I have told you all this so that in me you may find peace. In the world you will have suffering. But take heart! I have conquered the world' (REB). In the world we *will have suffering*, but because he has overcome the world *it* no longer has power to overcome us. Indeed, even in suffering, instead of being overwhelmed, we can have the healing virtue of inner peace.

Seeds of Suffering – Healing Fruit

To sum it up, the kind of person who is involved in pastoral care needs to impart a sense of spiritual and eternal hope to the sufferer. This is more likely to be achieved when the 'comfort' of Christ for the 'wounded healer' is fruitful, as it touches the life of another fellow sufferer. Being a wounded healer means knowing the healing presence of Christ in our own suffering. It also means being someone who knows the experience of being wounded by others' suffering. Both these aspects are the means whereby comfort is received from an eternal source. This source of comfort, because of its mysterious yet eternal value, is alive and passed on to others with whom it is shared. The seed of faith in suffering produces the life-giving fruit through the hope with which it is nurtured. 'Now faith is being sure of what we hope for and certain of what we do not see' (Hebrews 11.1 NIV).

Making It Better

This leads to another aspect of the challenge of pastoral involvement in suffering. Whether or not this is articulated, there is frequently expectation on behalf of both carer and sufferer that someone 'might/should' be able to take the suffering away. This is a human yearning and desire, but one which needs to be acknowledged and faced. Perhaps, therefore, one of the hardest things to come to terms with is when, in the here-and-now, we cannot take away or change another's suffering. Human nature can often find it more comfortable to be 'in control' rather than to feel out of control and useless. Our need as humans is to feel needed and to have a sense of achievement. It takes time and honesty to appreciate that being able to give to another something that is more spiritual and less tangible than activity (cure), is of a higher and a more eternal value. We might call this love. It is bearing the pain of 'being with' the sufferer, as opposed to being able to move on or away from the reality. It is in the sharing that there is the giving of the pastoral self, in comfort and sustenance. We give it in faith and with hope that it will remain. Hence the call to exercise faith, hope and love but the reminder that it is love which 'never ends' (1 Corinthians 13.8).

Suffering and the Growth of Creation

The crucial omission so far from our expositions is the lack of any substantial reference to the redemption which comes through Christ. To this we must come in due course. Before doing so, however, I propose to attempt a statement which, although clearly leaning towards the Irenaean view, will seek to bring together the central insights of both the Augustinian and Irenaean traditions.

In the discussion about suffering it is common for different words to be used almost synonymously and therefore confusingly. This is true in particular of the words 'pain', 'suffering' and 'evil'. The following statement will attempt partially to unhook these words, not in the sense that they never overlap and refer to the same reality (plainly sometimes they do), but in that they are not always to be identified. This is most easily shown by reflection upon the word 'pain'. Pain can be suffering and it can be evil but it is not inevitably either. It may fulfil a wholesome, though by definition painful, function. By extension of process of thought, granted that suffering is painful and that it often is evil, is it inevitably and inescapably evil, or are there some forms or moments of suffering which may indeed be good? The intention of this question is to unhook sin and suffering, and in particular to question the traditional assumption that what we call suffering cannot be part of God's created order and so must find some explanation which makes it, in the broadest sense, the consequence of human fallenness.

The Freedom of the Creation

These bald questions and bold statements must now be justified. I shall attempt to do so by taking up the notion of freedom which has become familiar to us through the free-will defence. We have seen that free human beings and free angelic creatures may both be identified as agents through which the irrationality of sin, rebellion against God and resistance to his gracious invitation to cooperation, enters God's creation. I want to extend this thought and to suggest the notion that creation itself, and not merely the personal agents within it, has a certain kind of freedom of its own. Admittedly, this needs to be differently conceived when we speak of subpersonal creation. We might think of it as a capacity for the unpredicted, the random or the spontaneous, which has been written into creation as part of that which enables it to grow and become. It is essentially a creative element. Creation has not been infinitely determined by God but is endowed by God with the capacity to bring forth from itself, to engage in a creative interaction with its Creator within the limits he sets for it.

We might say that God makes the *world* make itself, in that he creates the order and structure within which the inherent potential of the world he has created might unfold itself. In the creation narratives this is most clearly seen when God gives mandates to the various orders of creation to produce or to bring forth after their own kind. 'Creation' is God letting the world be, endowing it in its utter dependence on him with a relative freedom of its own. This implies on behalf of creaturely reality a capacity for spontaneity. It is as if the very mechanism which makes for variety and splendour is a certain randomness which throws up new possibilities and unheard-of diversity. It is the existence of uncertainty and un-predictability which, as any game of chance will show, when comprehended within a higher purpose and structure, fulfils an exciting and productive purpose. Randomness is not the same as chaos because it functions within a purposeful structure, but because it is essentially random neither can its effects be entirely controlled.

The implication of this position is that the very mechanism which serves the process of variation and development can produce that which falls short of the beautiful and the desir-able. Hence, a glorious creation exhibits inglorious traits and is capable of producing the brutal and the ugly which nevertheless have their place within the total variety of an interdependent creation.

The Role of Human Beings

The picture we have outlined enables us to conceive an evolutionary-developmental picture of creation in which the world realizes its potential not in independence from the Creator but through dependent interaction with him. It holds open the possibility that the Creator may speak creatively and anew into a world which is in process of becoming. Likewise it holds open the role of the personal creation as that part of creation which may with particular depth respond to its Maker. Humanity comes into being as personal being capable of profound and responsible response to the personal God. Human beings gather up and recapitulate the being of creation itself, being formed from the dust of the earth, being themselves akin to the animals – and yet more. They function in a priestly role within creation, summing up the response of inarticulate creation to the Creator and are potential mediators to creation of new depths of response to him. But when it fails to respond to God, humanity suppresses the response of creation and hinders it from rising beyond the conflict, which is a necessary stage of its free process of becoming, to that of cooperation.

Human freedom is also unpredictable and capable of misuse but because of the personal depth and responsibility of human creatures giving them the capacity to choose, what at the subpersonal level is a fact of existence becomes at the personal level culpable failure and sin. It is at this point that within an evolutionary-developmental framework it becomes possible to insert the concept of a Fall, a corporate and severe failure of humanity expressed by and in each person, to respond to the loving demands of the Creator. The consequence is to suppress the journey of creation towards its goal towards true and final liberty in corresponding fully to God. A joyful adventure is turned into a tragic deviation. It is because of this that the present creation may be said to be 'subject to frustration' and to 'groan as if in the pangs of childbirth' as it still awaits the 'glorious freedom of the children of God' (Romans 8.20–22).

The 'Dark Side' of Creation

The implications of this story of creation for suffering are as follows: God has created a finite world which is in process of development through, in part, the mechanism of random spontaneity. This mechanism is the source of untold good, but because it is truly random has a dark side. This dark side is productive of aspects of life which are painful, ugly and incomplete. This produces suffering. But the 'dark side' is not evil, it is merely dark. And the suffering it produces is not evil.

In human terms, the dark side of creation might be identified in experiences of pain, failure, disappointment, loss and the capacity for death. These elements may be seen as belonging to the 'shadow-side' of creation. They are not of themselves evil because these experiences play a particular role in the process of 'soul-making' and in entering into authentic personhood. Just as in the folk-tale the person who has no shadow does not exist, so in human growth shadow experiences serve to add personal depth to our being. They teach us to depend upon God and upon each other. They call forth the deeper resources of the human spirit. In this way even the shadow takes its rightful place in the good creation and is not to be feared. Some experiences of human suffering belong to the shadow and they are best not resented or received with bitterness but embraced as necessarily part of our journey. Yet it is recognized that they fall short of the blessedness which is our goal, that they are imperfect. If such experiences appear to conflict with our image of a loving God, it is because he is infinitely more wise than are we. He knows the end from the beginning, that is, he knows his own freedom to take the experiences that come our way and use them for this gracious purpose and the benefit which would accrue to us as a consequence. And the random experiences always take place within an overarching framework of purpose, even though it be hidden from us.

Pain, Mourning and Grief

What Nigel has said above about the 'dark side' of creation can be illustrated by the experiences of 'loss' in life. Such experiences are part of the natural web of life, and it is hard to see how at least some of them could be avoided even in an 'unfallen' creation. They lead to pain, mourning and grief. The pastoral issue is how to help someone go through such an experience and grow through it in a positive way.

The task is somehow to enable the sufferer to know the experience of the comfort of God for themselves and to mobilize their resources toward that end. We strive to gain an entry into the other's mind and inner self, in order that what we have to offer might be accessible. However, one person cannot actually get inside another and change either them or the situation around them. The pastoral task is a facilitating one. Another way in which we might understand this idea is to think of it as firstly making a correct diagnosis and *then* writing the prescription. But of course in writing a prescription we have to have a thorough working knowledge of the action of the drugs and their appropriate dosage and then to make the correct choice from the selection available. In the very end, the patient 'swallows the pill' or not. Our responsibility is for the best prescription, not for the patient's ultimate choice of taking the medicine or not.

What fulfilling this facilitating role means can best be illustrated by a concrete example, such as dealing with the issues of pain, mourning and grief.

Pain

As Nigel points out, it is helpful to remember that besides being a component of suffering, pain can often be a warning that something is wrong. It alerts us to the fact that an area of our being needs attention. For instance, the pain of an aching tooth is a form of suffering. However, it alerts us to the abscess, which is the actual cause although it may not at that time be visible. If this pain means that the abscess receives treatment and becomes healed, then the risk of the whole body being infected, with possible fatal consequences, has been avoided. So, as pain can have an alerting function, suffering can be a corrective force as it stimulates re-thinking, change of attitude and growth in personhood. This may apply in a physical, emotional, mental or spiritual sense.

Change and Loss

Coming now to the area of grief, it is a useful pastoral tool to have an understanding of the process which a human being endures following situations and circumstances of loss. We might broaden the concept of loss by adding to it ideas such as 'separation' and 'deprivation'. Disruption of any kind can result in a situation which brings suffering. In the normal cycle of life there may be new stages and phases which are welcomed. However, in welcoming the new we have to leave behind the old. The old, although in some ways we may be glad to leave it behind, nevertheless had that sense of familiarity and of security about it. The new takes an individual into the unknown, the untested, the untried. Therefore there is vulnerability and a sense of unknown in change, in spite of our welcome and high expectations of how it will treat us. Another point worthy of note with regard to experiences of change is that it is not only the person who is the focus of the change who is affected. We all live constantly in relationship to one another. Therefore a change in one person means that other people who are in relationship with that person may also involuntarily become part of that person's experience of suffering due to the change.

Natural Change

This dispersed effect of change must be noted and borne in mind in our pastoral work. 'Natural' or 'predictable' change occurs from birth, through childhood growth and development, leading on to school. From school years to leaving home. From the stage of marriage or singleness on into the midlife situation. From working life into retirement and finally to death. This is a bird's eye view of the normal kind of life cycle.

Pause for a moment or two though, and consider some of the familiarity and the security which is left behind in the moves from one stage to another. In addition, include those who are in relationship with the person undergoing change. We can then perhaps see how broadly grief and a sense of loss, separation and deprivation does range. These are what we might term the predictable changes. To some extent, they may be anticipated.

Unpredictable Changes

Additionally, all of us are subject to unpredictable changes. Situations such as illness, accident, disasters, marital separation, still-births, miscarriage, bereavement (loss of a person), financial, social and economical crises are all part of unpredictable change. One or more may occur at the same time as we are coping with some of the more predictable changes. Beside these we may add 'spiritual transitions'.

Spiritual Transitions

When people move on in their spiritual experience or embrace the Christian faith, there may well be certain lifestyles, priorities and attitudes which have to change. At one level the mind may understand that such change is appropriate. But at another level emotional attachments or dependencies may require relinquishment, in order for the new lifestyle or attitude to become truly effective.

The Grief Journey

Grief is often described as a journey. For purposes of description, and to help it become meaningful, it is divided into *stages* of experience. This should not detract from the fact that a grief pathway is an individual one. It is unpredictable, may keep a person for a longer time in one stage than another and may indeed oscillate between stages. Descriptive words and the use of stages are for the purposes of an understanding, to create a tool with which to help a person on the journey. It should not be taken as a strait-jacket into which a person must fit or is otherwise seen to be abnormal. I shall describe this process here very briefly. Those who are interested in studying it more fully will need to equip themselves with other material and training which is available. This is only a pointer to alert readers to this aspect of the pastoral challenge in the face of suffering.

(a) Stage One is often described as a state of numbness, shock, disbelief, denial. (Note: we may also hear 'it is too good to be true', in happy, welcomed events). The outer changes are more than our 'inner world', for the time being, can fully absorb and cope with. The situation at this stage can leave the victim as it were on 'auto-pilot'. This in fact is a mechanism of defence and of protection which is graciously built within us. We are wise to recognize this, for example in relation to a bereaved person's behaviour before and during a funeral. Such a person may appear to be coping well and we might be glad within ourselves to conclude that they are managing. (Generally speaking, we are not awfully comfortable with dealing with facing loss and death!) The reality is that the shock, the demands, the decisions, arrangements and preparations have simply not yet given opportunity for the auto-pilot to sense that it may switch off. Real grief may have scarcely begun, leave alone have been completed!

(b) Stage Two might perhaps be captioned with the phrase 'if only'. Words such as 'yearning', 'searching', 'pining' may be apt. If we liken the grief journey to travelling through a dark tunnel, then we set off at the beginning and have to complete the largest portion of the route before light comes into view. The journey up to that point, in the natural sense, is in the dark. Illumination is by artificial light. Often people find the feelings and experiences of the grief journey something like this. The 'if only' cry so often uttered, indicates that the beginning of the tunnel is closer than its end. So 'if only' I had not done that or this had not happened. In essence, if by reasoning the situation away – it did not exist – then the bewilderment and pain which is experienced would not exist or be real either! There is the sense of a 'gap', but time has not yet allowed the reality of its cause to fully dawn. So, coming to terms with the status quo and making the necessary adjustments and adaptations is not possible for the agenda as yet.

(c) Stage Three is reached when more reality is now dawning and feelings therefore can seem more powerfully alive. They can also give a sense of not being controllable. Rather *they* seem to be in control of the person who grieves. These feelings will be those such as of anger, depression, guilt, frustration and will be powerful emotions. They may not be easy to 'place' in the mind and understanding of the sufferer. They may well be 'displaced' on to persons and situations which in reality are not appropriate. It may be that decisions to make quite radical and significant changes would seem to be the answer at this time. However, decisions such as to move house, or to take legal action against the person(s) upon whom the blame appears to rest, are better discouraged than encouraged at this stage. The fact of the loss is becoming more real but the grief journey remains incomplete, adjustment has not yet been accomplished. So there can be strong moves considered to change or undo this overwhelming pain which is the experience of the grieving. Because the emotions are mainly in control, the mind has difficulty in behaving rationally. This can be a painful and bewildering experience for the sufferer. The pastoral carer has to cling to the role of 'enabler', and not try to be a 'make it better' doer.

(d) Stage Four is hopefully the stage of acceptance and adjustment. Regrettably, this stage can arrive without healing, with bitterness and resentment, perhaps anger (often displaced onto another person or situation) still there, leaving a person unhealed with long-term wounds. When situations or relationships linked with the loss are unresolved, the traveller may become stuck in the tunnel. For example, a state of redundancy resulting in diminished finance and lifestyle; a death occurring before broken relationships have been restored.

This, of course, is what we are seeking to avoid in the improved understanding and skill of helping those who grieve. A part of the healing experience may be to enable the unresolved to be peacefully and effectively dealt with, along the journey. Remember, though, we cannot get inside another person and make the changes ourselves. Time sometimes has to be part of the healing process. To be faithful, and to equip ourselves and do our best is our duty. Where there has been a journey experiencing healing and personal growth, then the loss becomes an accepted fact and creative adjustments have been and continue to be made.

Nonetheless, it remains important to understand that this stage does not mean an absence of painful feelings or memories. Such may continue and be triggered unexpectedly or irrationally. The essence of evidence of healing is that although pain still arises, the person concerned is in good control of the emotions; rather than continuing to be overwhelmed and controlled *by* the pain of grief. This may be a helpful summary of the purpose and aims of this inevitable grief.

The Grief Tasks

The tasks that need to be undertaken, and hopefully completed successfully, when dealing with grief can briefly be summarized as follows.

- To enable the sufferer to accept the reality of loss.
- To help the person to work through the inevitable pain of grief.

- To encourage the griever to adjust to an environment in which that which *is* lost is still missing.
- To encourage emotional relocation from that which is lost and to move on with life.

In other words, to withdraw the emotional energy from the process of grieving and to reinvest it in the adjusting to the new situation.

Suffering, Sin and Evil

We have made a case for saying that some suffering comes to us not as a result of human fallenness and sin but as a consequence of our finitude, our createdness within a world in process of becoming. It is part of the fabric of reality. This, not surprisingly, leaves many questions open of which the largest must be not why there is *some* suffering but why there is so much, and why it is often so meaningless. Having attempted to unhook suffering and sin, what are we to say about the link between them?

Fallen Beings

Human beings are undoubtedly fallen. The effects of this in relation to suffering are twofold. Because we are alienated from God we deprive ourselves of the very resources we need for our natural sufferings to be transfigured. Sufferings, natural to our finitude, which might be taken up through our communion with God and transformed into blessedness, are instead endured in anxiety, fear and isolation. In this sense fallenness is at the root of our *experience* of suffering. Furthermore, it is through sin that malice, hatred and exploitation enter into human experience. So to the natural sufferings which we have called the 'shadow' there is added an 'unnatural' (in the sense that it does not belong to the good structure of creation) reality of suffering which is to be attributed directly to sin, the misuse of our creaturely freedom. It is here that the word 'evil' may truly be attributed to such sufferings.

Because human existence is inherently corporate, so these sufferings are inevitably 'unjust' in that there is no easy correlation between individual sin and its consequences. People, and most especially the weak and vulnerable, suffer because of the sins of others and the corporate injustices of human social systems. Protest against such evil becomes inevitably part of our Christian experience at this point. If Christians struggle against the product of the 'shadow-side' of the good creation by reason of its imperfection, how much more should they struggle against that which is truly evil! At all points Christians strive to alleviate suffering, but at no point more so than when that suffering is clearly seen to be hostile to the very nature and purpose of creation. Our difficulty is in learning to disentangle what belongs to the shadow from what is unambiguously evil. This is not an easy task, but a broken arm is clearly of a different order from a malignant growth.

The Work of Christ

So far we have attempted to understand why things are as they are, and why they are necessarily so. Our reflection would not however be complete without understanding the matter in the light of Christ. The Christian confesses that God has acted lovingly and savingly in Christ. How, in reference to suffering, might this be deemed to be the case?

We suggested above that some dimensions of what we call suffering might belong to our existence as created, finite and questing beings. There is a long-standing debate in Christian theology as to whether the incarnation was rendered necessary as the remedy for sin, the presupposition of the cross, or whether even in an unfallen world the Son of God would have become incarnate as the expression of God's creative grace. In the light of what has been claimed above, it is possible to argue that even apart from sin the incarnation would have happened as God's means of sharing in the creative suffering of his world. In that way he would show himself not to be apart and not to be exempt from the world's struggle to become. Indeed, God's participation in this way in creaturely existence may also be the means whereby the world is moved on towards its ultimate goal of correspondence with God. At one level, we are able to see this significance in the drama of Christ's incarnation.

However, the actual form of Christ's incarnation, his coming to die in identification with humankind and under judgement, must be seen to be shaped by creation's need, specifically humankind's need, to be redeemed from sin. In that sense, in incarnation

Christ enters not only the natural suffering of created existence but the unnatural and unjust suffering of fallen creation. In doing so he overcomes evil and injustice by bearing the onslaughts of both and absorbing their powerful hostility. In this Christ acts as representative of God and of humanity itself. The resurrection is both the sign of Christ's victory over evil and of God's activity within the totality of human existence whereby he is overcoming evil and injustice and will through Christ and in the Spirit bringing creation to its own day of final transformation and healing.

In this confession are both comfort and realism. Comfort in that there is a promise of final healing and renewal. Realism in that this is emphatically 'not yet'. It is *through* many tribulations that we are to enter the Kingdom of Heaven. What faith in Christ offers therefore is not escape from this world's sufferings – certainly not from those which belong to the good shadow, but also not from that evil suffering which derives from sin and fall. Yet it does offer a faith with which to pass through that suffering, the presence of one who has passed through it himself, and a hope that all things will be transfigured in resurrection glory. In addition it gives the model of one who exercised a costly and relentless ministry to overcome evil and relieve suffering in all its forms. None of these gracious gifts may be despised. And if resurrection beyond death remains the fundamental pattern of our existence, there are also inklings and anticipations from time to time within the mortal creation of the resurrection power and glory that belong to the future. These are sometimes called 'miracles'. It may be more helpful to see them as 'signs' since they exist as much in the seeing as in objective fact; graciously given indicators of the future that God is to bring.

The Scriptures offer us a vision of a new heaven and a new earth. Those who believe live in hope of this vision, not in the sense that they wish to escape from the present world, but in the hope that the present creation and all within it will be set free from its bondage to decay. Jürgen Moltmann has a fine vision of such a future when he speaks of the 'divine tempest of the new creation, which sweeps out of God's future over history's fields of the dead, waking and gathering every last created being'.[1] In such a vision there is a brave and confident hope which strengthens us in the realities of our current lot.

Pastoral Pointers

Finally, what pointers might be given to the pastoral application of the train of thought developed here? We should encourage people to believe that:

(a) Life contains necessary pain and struggle which should be accepted without resentment but with courage and the determination to grow through all experiences. The answer to the question 'Why me?' is sometimes just 'That's life'; in other words: God is not singling out people for punishment, they are simply sharing in the common lot of humanity. Yet this apparent randomness is foreseen, known and comprehended by the loving and all-wise God so that it is by no means the outworking of impersonal fate.

(b) Life also contains the assaults of evil which are the product of the world's resistance to God. Faith in Christ is the supreme resource for enduring such assaults. It offers a confident hope but no guarantee of exemption from the struggle. The cross and resurrection show that even the worst of events can be used for ultimate good by the infinitely creative God. Despite the fact that they contain no intrinsic logic they can be made to serve a purpose against their nature.

(c) People need help in disentangling what is happening to them and being able to identify and name and so to a degree confront and make sense of their suffering. Some of the experience of suffering concerns how we relate and respond to the things that happen to us. Wise pastoral work at this point can relieve suffering even if the outward circumstances remain unchanged.

(d) The Christian imitates Christ in compassion for the suffering and works with him in costly but resolute determination to overcome all forms of evil and its effects not least by being present for others in their suffering.

Facing the Pastoral Challenge

In this final part of the chapter we will build on Nigel's 'pointers' for pastoral application as we consider the pastoral challenges of seeking to imitate Christ in helping those who face suffering. Perhaps the first thing to say is that although we have tools of theology, an understanding of different experiences of suffering, training and even compassion, they all need to be used in the order and manner which is best suited to the sufferer, in the 'now'. In other words, there is no pre-set order in either value or priority in which these tools are used. In addition to all this, our reliance upon, and sensitivity to, the Holy Spirit of God as we listen is always of paramount importance. In this connection we reiterate that although any two persons' experience may *appear* the same, their form of suffering will have its unique individuality. A priority therefore always is to 'listen' to how it feels for the person concerned, the effects, influences, thoughts and reactions which it triggers. The so-called 'Job's Comforters' were ineffective in their pastoral task because they sought to give Job *their* perspective of his suffering, rather than truly hear and empathize with *his* perspective!

Addressing the protest. The question 'Why me?' is a very common one and appears in varied forms. As Nigel says, it is usually not a request for a theological answer but a protest. It is also a cry for release from the pain. It can reflect a refusal to accept the reality of the suffering, or the situation that causes it. At this point the pastor's task may simply be to offer empathy and compassion, sharing something of the comfort learnt through being a 'wounded healer'. As the sufferer is given the time and permission to talk, the reality of the situation and the suffering will come to be accepted.

Prayer. As we listen to and begin to understand the sufferer's point of view our prayer will become more informed and relevant. Even so, as we pray that God, through the Holy Spirit, will use the care and compassion we offer to open the heart of the sufferer to receive his comfort and strength, we will sometimes need to ask the Spirit to pray on our behalf, because we do not know what to pray (Romans 8.26–27).

Suffering and sin. In our theological reflection we have clarified that suffering is by no means to be automatically seen as the consequence of the sufferer's sin. However, honesty sometimes must lead us to admit that, in part at least, in some situations this is so. The God of healing and wholeness whom we seek to serve and represent, while loving sinners, does hate sin. An aspect of the pastoral task must therefore be to enable confession and repentance, when appropriate.

Drawing attention to sin, where necessary, is a loving act. It is a wrong sort of compassion which allows us to be coerced into ignoring sin, or denying as sin that which is sinful. The drawing attention to sin is part of the process of disentangling and confronting the situation of the sufferer of which Nigel speaks. It must, of course, be done in a spirit of humility and not self-righteousness. It is more likely to be accepted when compassionate caring has already been demonstrated.

Forgiveness. The sufferer may have been wronged, in reality or perception, and this may add to the pain of the situation. Why are we instructed to forgive one another? Partly in order to release the offender, but also partly for the healing of the offended. St Paul speaks of not letting sin have dominion over us (Romans 6.12). Does not this include sin committed *against us*? Our natural (fallen) reaction to being sinned against is to have a sense of revenge, to hold grudges and become bitter, but these can cause suffering in their own way. Forgiveness removes the consequences of being sinned against from the sufferer's life. Jesus sets us the supreme example of the sufferer forgiving those who caused his suffering. He was put to death unjustly, yet prayed for the forgiveness of those who caused his pain, 'Father, forgive them; for they do not know what they are doing' (Luke 23.34).

It is sometimes very difficult to forgive. In such situations it helps to recognize that forgiveness can be a *process*. Initially there can be partial forgiveness. This can create a space for the forgiver and the forgiven to receive something of God's love and peace, which then provides the resources to continue the process towards its completion. To return to a metaphor we used earlier, it is like planting a seed of forgiveness, which can then grow. God, I believe, blesses the will to forgive the offender, even when putting that into practice takes time. Because it is often a process, forgiving and forgetting do not always go together. However, what matters is the *attitude* with which we remember – whether it is one of bitterness or of forgiveness.

Suffering and evil. Evil, in varied forms, does seem to invade people's lives. We are not able to discuss here the matter of 'deliverance' from evil as part of healing ministry. We can only make some brief observations. Those who are pastorally involved with people would be wise to learn and develop discernment in this area so as to be able to make a correct diagnosis of the kind of help that a sufferer needs. It might be helpful to look at it in the following way. Someone may periodically suffer from inflammation in a finger. Eventually it is realized that there is an infective splinter in the finger. Until it is removed all efforts at lasting healing will be thwarted. It may be like this for some people on the spiritual and moral level. There is some evil source of the suffering in their life which needs to be removed before there can be true healing. However, 'deliverance', in whatever form it may take, is not all that is needed. As in the case of the splinter, after-care is still needed to bring about the final healing of the wound left after the source of the suffering is removed.

Imitating Christ. The pastoral challenge may seem such a daunting task that we wonder whether or not we can cope with it. It is just at this point that we need to make sure that we continue to imitate Christ. How did Jesus cope? The Gospels show us that he was aware of a draining of energy and resources as he gave himself in healing to others (Mark 5.30). There seem to be at least four things which he did which enabled him to cope with this.

1. He consulted his heavenly Father as he decided the detail of his 'workload' (Mark 1.35).

2. Having concluded what his Father's will was for the day, he fulfilled this, not in his own strength but by the power of the Holy Spirit (Matthew 12.28), and through prayer he replenished his resources (Matthew 14.23).

3. He had friends, carefully chosen, with whom he shared his human needs and relaxed and ate, 'fellowshipping' with them.

4. He taught and trained others and delegated work to them, so that they worked alongside him and then were able to carry on his work after he had left this earth.

We continue that work which Jesus delegated to his disciples. However, we need to remember that the final 'burden' of the work rests on him, not us. Like the hands in the picture described earlier, we must let him support us as we minister to the suffering. He is the ultimate source of the healing that they need.

References

1. J. Moltmann, *The Way of Jesus Christ: Christology in Messianic Dimensions* (London, SCM 1990), p. 303.

Further Reading

THEOLOGY:

J.A. Baker, *The Foolishness of God*, Fontana
P.S. Fiddes, *The Creative Suffering of God*, OUP
J. Hick, *Evil and the God of Love*, Fontana
C.S. Lewis, *The Problem of Pain*, Fontana
J. Moltmann, *The Crucified God*, SCM

THE EXPERIENCE OF SUFFERING:

A.V. Campbell, *The Gospel of Anger*, SPCK
S. Cassidy, *Light from the Dark Valley*, DLT
S. Cassidy, *Sharing the Darkness*, DLT
H. Nouwen, *Seeds of Hope*, DLT
H. Nouwen, *The Way of the Heart*, DLT
M. Wilson, *A Coat of Many Colours*, Epworth

SUPPORT FOR PASTORAL CARERS:

M.A. Coate, *Clergy Stress*, SPCK
J. Foskett and D. Lyall, *Helping the Helpers*, SPCK
Other books in the SPCK New Library of Pastoral Care are also
    worth consulting.

ISSUES OF GRIEF:

J. Grigor, *Loss – An Invitation to Grow*, Arthur James
C.S. Lewis, *A Grief Observed*, Fontana
P. Sampson, *The Courage to Hope*, SU
A.M. Smith, *Gateway to Life*, IVP
W. Worden, *Grief Counselling and Grief Therapy*, Routledge

EVIL AND DELIVERANCE MINISTRY:

M. Green, *I Believe in Satan's Downfall*, Hodder and Stoughton
R. Parker, *The Occult*, IVP
M. Perry, *Deliverance*, SPCK
N.G. Wright, *The Fair Face of Evil*, Marshall Pickering

CHAPTER 6

Psychiatry and Religion

———

Dr C. V. Russell Blacker
Revd Beaumont Stevenson

Mental illness is a large and complex subject. In the consultation process we at first decided that it was too big a topic to be dealt with alongside the rest of our agenda. However, we eventually decided that it was too important, and too often neglected when considering the Church's healing ministry, for us to ignore it. Given the limitations of time, it could only be dealt with in a fairly general way. We concentrated on the general subject of the problems and possibilities for cooperation between Christian pastoral carers and psychiatrists. We were fortunate to be able to draw into the consultation a consultant psychiatrist and a chaplain working in a mental hospital, both with a great deal of experience in the area of mental health care.

Psychiatry and Religion:
A Psychiatrist's View

There is a long-standing distrust between psychiatry and religion which has often been to the detriment of members of religious communities who develop psychological problems.

Throughout this chapter I use the term 'religion' as a shorthand for religious activity as shown by specifically *Christian* commitment. The term 'psychiatry' is used in a similarly generic fashion to indicate the typical clinical activities of psychiatrists and other mental health professionals working within the British National Health Service system.

It is important to recognize that such professionals are principally concerned with the diagnosis and treatment of the more *severe* mental illnesses such as: schizophrenia, manic-depression, dementia, depression, and so on. They are not, by and large, heavily involved with the normal turmoil and distress associated with life's difficulties (such as bereavement and broken relationships) unless it leads to complications such as taking an overdose, although members of community teams and those running so-called 'crisis services' will probably do so. Of course there is no clear-cut distinction between normal and abnormal reactions to life's difficulties and decisions. Whether such reactions are normal or morbid is a clinical and arbitrary one. In reality the decision is usually made by the referring General Practitioner in consultation with the patient.

Clergy and counsellors within the Church setting will see a good proportion of those who develop more normal reactions to stress, but not exclusively so. Patients with severe psychiatric illness will attend church, and depression, in particular, is a common and serious condition which often escapes detection by clergy, relatives, and even the G.P. Non-detection results in non-treatment, often with disastrous consequences and a great deal of prolonged suffering for the patient and their family. There are many reasons for this, but one of them is a mutual conspiracy to avoid labelling someone as mentally ill and a wish to 'protect' them from having to see a psychiatrist.

Christian Distrust of Psychiatry

There is already a great deal of stigma towards the mentally ill in our society, but in religious circles this can be amplified by additional fears that consulting a doctor for psychological problems betrays a lack of faith. Those with mental problems may even be *discouraged* by others within the Church from seeking help out of a misplaced fear that their religious belief will be dismissed by the psychiatrist or seen as a manifestation of neurosis and subject to a programme of 'treatment' to remove it. This fear stems from a further misunderstanding (common in the general public) that psychiatry is all about psychoanalysis, and Freudian atheistical reductionist psychoanalysis in particular. Although Freud made many important observations about the functioning of the human mind his contribution to everyday clinical psychiatry in the 1990s is almost non-existent and psychoanalysis as a form of treatment is now largely disregarded.

Psychiatrists nowadays are taught to respect their patients' beliefs and value systems, which ought to mean that Christians who are referred to psychiatrists who are not themselves believers should have nothing to fear. A good psychiatrist will want to become aware of the patient's beliefs and build upon them as far as they are constructive and potentially therapeutic or personally affirming. This may well necessitate an interview with the patient's religious leader and/or an invitation for assistance in the form of religious support and counselling while they are receiving psychiatric treatment. However, it is important to be aware that religious beliefs can be used in a defensive or harmful way. This is sometimes seen in requests by Christian patients to see specifically Christian psychiatrists hoping, by this means, to escape being asked embarrassing (but important) questions about their private life, or to avoid being challenged over certain maladaptive behaviours. In some circumstances the Christian patient may derive *more* benefit from seeing an excellent non-believing psychiatrist than a less experienced Christian one.

Psychiatrists' Misunderstanding of Religion

There are also misunderstandings within *psychiatry* towards religious faith. Although the old Freudian notion that religious faith was itself a manifestation of neurosis – a defence against underlying conflicts and anxieties – has weakened, this process has been slowed by the fact that most psychiatrists' contact with religion comes in the form of religious *casualties*. One thinks of the strange and bizarre religious beliefs held by those who are psychotic, the ecstatic outpourings of those in the grip of mania or the deep convictions of guilt unworthiness and damnation in the severely depressed. In other, less dramatic, cases religious beliefs may be inextricably tied up with, and distorted by, problems lying within the patient's personality and/or unresolved conflicts from the past which have taken on a religious disguise; for example, the abused child who goes on to develop a simultaneous fear and need for a father which is then projected onto the Father God and/or other 'father figures' in the Church hierarchy. Psychiatrists and other mental health professionals seldom have the opportunity to see religious faith in its healthy normative mode, a problem compounded by the fact that it is still not expected of psychiatrists to make a systematic examination of their patient's religious commitment when taking their history. Sadly, psychiatrists know very little about religious development and growth, how to tell normal from pathological religious belief, and how to examine for it and correct it.

With the debunking of religion, psychiatry lost much of the insight and understanding that went with it. The result is that psychiatry has very little to say about the *nature* of Man. Although psychiatric textbooks and psychotherapy manuals have plenty to say about the workings of the human mind they have nothing to say about *who* or *what* Man is. Psychiatry has also ignored the possibility that behaviour might have *moral* value, with positive or negative spiritual consequences and potentially harmful effects upon the personality. It has also been totally unable to provide a satisfactory explanation for the existence and meaning of suffering and has nothing to say about what happens when we die, whether we have souls or whether God exists. This is because psychiatry, in common with the physical sciences, became separated from religion in the nineteenth century and has pursued a separate path ever since. Psychiatry and religion therefore speak different languages and have evolved quite different scientific methodologies.

Each discipline's methodology, which is reflected in its language, is quite appropriate for its particular task. Psychiatry's language is the language of phenomenological description – the description of symptoms and signs of disorder. This is wholly appropriate for its job of healing the sick. But this language and methodology is quite inappropriate for the task of establishing whether God exists or whether we can be influenced by invisible spirit beings. Religious inquiry is the right instrument for resolving such questions. However, we have inherited a misconception that religious statements are invalid because they cannot be measured or subjected to laboratory analysis. (In fact this is not strictly true; one can observe some religious truths while a good many psychiatric experiences, such as hallucination, can equally be said to be 'non-verifiable'). This misconception remains unchallenged because one methodology – the incorrect one as it happens – is inappropriately applied to the data generated by another, quite unrelated, discipline. It is as though one should attempt to dismantle a car engine with the help of a cookery book. Religious methodology is every bit as credible and 'scientific' (if you like) within its own sphere of expertise as is psychiatry's within its sphere of mental illness. Psychiatrists cannot therefore tell you whether fallen angels exist and religion cannot tell you how to cure schizophrenia, or why people get it – despite the enthusiastic claims of some people.

We thus have a state of affairs in which those in religious circles are largely ignorant of the potential benefits of psychiatry whilst psychiatrists and their colleagues are unaware of the potential benefits of grace and faith. The root cause is the historical separation of psychiatry and religion and the independent evolution of different languages and methodologies to describe mental and spiritual phenomena. There is thus a dialogue of the deaf which serves only to entrap the seriously unwell or spiritually famished in a continuing state of wretchedness and adversity. Of course there are good and bad churches just as there are good and bad psychiatrists and one of the benefits of a little knowledge in both directions is the ability to know when each is being harmful rather than beneficial.

Signs of Improvement

Fortunately, the situation is changing for the better. Within religious circles there has been a growing awareness of the need to understand and help those with psychological problems. This is demonstrated in the rise of the pastoral counselling service which finds expression in many ways:

- hospital chaplains appointed to mental health units.
- formal religious counselling training programmes and centres for religious counselling and healing.
- a veritable deluge of self-help books and autobiographies
- a widespread trend towards teaching and preaching which is more *person*-centred and less exclusively 'doctrinal'.
- the establishment in many churches of regular weekly fellowship groups and personal counselling and healing teams.
- most Bible Colleges and Theological Seminaries also now have a core curriculum which includes basic psychology and psychiatry.

In addition there are specialist organizations, such as the Association for the Pastoral Care of the Mentally Ill, which aim to educate and equip churches to support those in their midst who are sufferiing from *severe* mental illnesses. There are splendid examples of Christian treatment centres for those suffering from drug and alcohol dependency. There are, moreover, several voluntary organizations working closely *with* psychiatry (such as the Manic-Depression

Fellowship and Alcoholics Anonymous) which have an explicitly (although not exclusively) religious basis.

There are also changes within psychiatry itself. Back in the early 1960s in the United Kingdom an association of Christian psychiatrists existed which had only a handful of members; now the daughter organization has over 220 members (approximately 6 per cent of all psychiatrists in the country) and is growing fast. A recent survey of psychiatrists in London teaching hospitals revealed that 40 per cent believe in God and 20 per cent attend church on a regular weekly basis.

Healing and the Church – Striking a Balance

Nonetheless, there is room for improvement and certain criticisms can be made. In some religious circles so great has the enthusiasm been for counselling and pastoral care that the original spiritual mandate to teach the word of God and manifest the fruits of the Spirit have become quite neglected. At worst this leads to a state of affairs in which the Church of God has become transformed into a social services department or a rather amateur form of psychiatric day centre. The social gospel *is* important but never so important that it should be allowed to assume pre-eminence over evangelism to the unbeliever or giving the people of God their primary nourishment . . . the Word of God as taught to them in a dedicated and responsible way.

We live in a society of increasing religious disillusionment, spiritual ignorance and moral decay, much of the responsibility for which must go to the Church and its retreat from the important task of doing what God commanded it to do. It has been said somewhat facetiously that Jesus came to this earth to found a kingdom; instead he got the Church! There are sections of the Church – particularly the charismatic house church groups – which have launched an aggressive counter-attack to this spiritual decay by offering a largely *experiential* faith with healing as a central feature. Whereas the impact of these churches has been far more beneficial than otherwise there is the danger of healing becoming an end in itself and of thereby cultivating a faith which is shallow and immature, depending as it does upon regular 'shots' of excitement provided by the new pseudo-apostles of our age. Healing should never become a central feature of our Christian faith, it is a side-effect of contact with God. In the New Testament it is normally linked with the proclamation of the gospel.

My suspicion is that a lot of the current enthusiasm for healing ministries has less to do with exploring the gifts of the Holy Spirit than with current difficulties in dealing with the problem of *suffering*. The charismatic healing ministries have developed in the context of a materialistic culture in which suffering is seen as failure, in which there is a thirst for quick over-the-counter solutions to difficult problems and in which religions that are seen to 'work' are also those that 'sell' well. Secondly, our culture is also influenced by a scientific mode of thinking in which only that which is *consciously* experienced (and reverifiable in scientific experiment) is regarded as valid. Faith, and the walk of faith, is an early casualty in this sort of intellectual climate and it is a natural temptation to want to prove to a disbelieving world that our religion is not an exercise of our imagination. Yet there is a third, paradoxical, counter-influence behind the current obsession with the miraculous which stems from a deep distrust of the control exercised by professionals who are the high priests of the scientific culture. Hence the rise of alternative medicine and hence, also, I suspect, the rise of our healing ministries.

Healing and the Church – Some Problems

There is a disagreeable side to some of the modern healing ministries which needs to be exposed. Firstly, many of the claims of healing are pseudo-healing, the temporary suppression of symptoms and pain associated with diseases in the context of deliberately engineered emotional excitement (not unlike some of the shamanistic practices of witch doctors in tribal Africa and elsewhere). All too often symptoms return a few days later, although by then the itinerant guru has moved on and the local church is left (sometimes literally) to pick up the pieces. In the case of mental illness or of those who are unstable mentally the results can be devastating, the effect enhanced by the added implication that a return of symptoms betrays a lack of 'faith'.

The psychiatrist is able to contribute to solving this difficulty through their understanding of the phenomenon of 'dissociation'. Dissociation is a mental process in which conscious and unconscious thoughts and feelings become split off from one another.

146

Patients who dissociate are capable of acting at variance with the known facts, thus giving rise to the phenomena of post-hypnotic suggestion: fictitious illness, psychosomatic disorders or (in the case of pseudo-healing) suppression of physical symptoms. The reference to hypnosis reminds us that we are all subject to the power of suggestion to one degree or another, and dissociation is especially likely to occur where people's suggestibility is exploited, for example through emotional excitement and contact with other similarly excited people. An important recent example of the phenomenon of dissociative pseudo-healing at work was demonstrated in a televized follow-up by Dr Peter May of fourteen cases of 'healing' from a Morris Cerullo rally. On occasion the exploitation of dissociative processes in mass healing rallies can lead to psychiatric breakdown. A previous follow-up by myself and Dr Margaret Hodson of eleven 'casualties' of a John Wimber rally in the 1970s identified two such cases which required admission to hospital.

Psychiatrists and allied professionals are in a position to identify the sociological significance of these activities. An important study by the late E. Mansell Pattison (a devout Christian and Professor of Psychiatry in the USA) showed that so-called 'healing' rituals often constitute an exploitation of the sick (the subjects) for the purpose of increasing the faith of the well (the audience).[1] This is repugnant on several counts.

- First, it is dishonest. Patients are being invited to expect physical healing when this does not in fact occur.
- Second, the common practice of redesignating any subsequent emotional benefits as a form of 'inner healing' is a side-stepping technique and also deceitful.
- Third, God is not glorified by human attempts to reproduce the divine. True miraculous healings (which do occur and are documented) are being obscured and robbed of their proper evangelistic impact by false but strident claims arising from large numbers of pseudo-healings.

Healing and the Church – Demon Possession

Closely related to healing ministries is the issue of demon possession. Psychiatrists occasionally come across patients from religious

147

backgrounds who have developed a straightforward psychiatric disorder but which has been mistakenly 'diagnosed' as demonic in origin by members of their own church. In some instances this has resulted in repeated and unnecessary attempts at exorcism, leading on to serious decompensation or even suicide. The presence of a diagnosable psychiatric disorder does not, of course, invalidate a possible spiritual basis or trigger for the disturbance itself but there is a tendency for *over-spiritualization* where there is a vacuum of ignorance. Many people, including sufferers themselves, find mental illness hard to understand and at times frightening. It is easy in this context to attribute symptoms and disturbed behaviour to some outside influence. This can lead to a delay in getting proper psychiatric help with all the attendant complications (such as failed marriage, loss of job, even loss of faith, etc) which that brings.

The Christian psychiatrist has much to offer in helping break down this barrier of ignorance, in alleviating fears concerning misdiagnosis or the rubbishing of spiritual issues, and (hopefully) by providing a programme of care that is offered in love and with the best interests of the patient at heart. Christian patients often ask to see a Christian psychiatrist. Sadly, this is not always possible because of the nature of their condition which requires ongoing, community-based, treatment and the need for the local consultant to be part of the team. Choice is therefore usually restricted by geography. However, being a Christian does not automatically make a doctor a better psychiatrist, and at the end of the day it is usually better for the patient to see a competent non-Christian psychiatrist than a less competent (or less experienced) Christian one. That is the advice I always give to those who ask whether they can see a Christian psychiatrist. Of course, where geography, religious orientation and competence combine, the patient is in a fortunate position.

Healing and Psychiatry – Understanding Belief

I have suggested that the Church has a long way to go before it is ready to understand psychiatry. Psychiatry, too, has a long way to go before it is ready to arrive at a happy working relationship with the spiritual. Psychiatrists are exposed to what other people *believe* at a fairly fundamental level but as yet psychiatry has no language with which to tackle 'belief' outside of that which automatically assumes a pathological disorder. As I have already said, the diagnosis of psychiatric disorder does not invalidate a possible spiritual basis or trigger for a particular condition. Psychiatry lacks the equipment to diagnose spiritual disorders and so is not able to detect problems and ensure that the patient is receiving the best care. Truly spiritual disorder may thus be mislabelled as psychological.

This over-medicalization is the mirror-image of the over-spiritualization seen in some religious groups. Once again it is facilitated by a vacuum of ignorance and, clearly, both psychiatrists and religious groups would benefit from regular interchange of information. Hambidge has calculated that the average consultant psychiatrist in the United Kingdom will have in the catchment area population he/she serves at least 5,500 practising church attenders, thirty-eight Christian churches and thirty supervising ministers.[2] Conversely, extrapolating from national epidemiological data most ministers of religion will have congregations in which approximately 12 per cent of the people will suffer from psychiatric disorder at some point in their lives. Hambidge also conducted a survey of fifty-four Theological Colleges and Bible Schools and forty-one University Departments of Psychiatry and Mental Hospitals. He found that whereas 69 per cent of theological training courses contain some sort of module on psychology/psychiatry (and most of those which didn't indicate a desire to have one) only 12 per cent of the *psychiatric* training schemes included teaching about religious practices. The danger in proposing psychiatric explanations for disturbances which have a spiritual basis is that it creates an antithesis between scientific and religious thought which does not actually exist. Psychiatry does not have all of the answers and there are important areas which are quite outside of its remit.

There is thus a considerable amount that psychiatrists can do in response to this situation at a *practical* level:

- forge links with local churches.
- become actively involved in teaching about mental illness in theological colleges and churches.
- form psychiatric teams willing to work in conjunction with experts in the *spiritual* field in the case of selected patients.

Psychiatrists need to become aware of the normal processes of religious development and to realize that there is a stage of spiritual maturation *beyond* secular humanism which is common to *them*

149

as well as their patients. Psychiatrists and psychotherapists need to move away from the notion of a person as a closed independent system to one in which the true interactions between people and between a person and God is recognized. The healing of society is critically dependent upon our ability to rediscover the importance of spirituality, and psychiatrists have as much a responsibility towards this as teachers and the media.

Much more of current psychiatric epidemiological research should examine patients' religious commitment and see whether this has a bearing upon outcome from various disorders such as depression. A recent analysis of all the scientific papers published in four major psychiatric journals (including the British Journal of Psychiatry) between 1978 and 1982 revealed that only 2.5 per cent bothered to inquire about religious variables and almost all of those were 'static' measures of religion rather than dynamic measures of religious belief.[3] As a consequence psychiatry knows relatively little about the possible dynamic effects of religious commitment on mental health. At the same time Dr David Larson (himself a distinguished epidemiologist) and his colleagues of the National Institute for Health Care Research have been successful in identifying that where research has included religious variables they are often positively associated with measures of health and mental health.[4]

Where Can We Go From Here?

Apart from implementing the above suggestions regarding training and forging practical clinical links between psychiatry and the churches, there are specific skills which psychiatry and religion each have which, if properly applied, will enhance the quality of the service being provided by the other. In the case of the churches these devolve into:

- awareness of the principle psychiatric disorders, the main ways in which they become apparent, and what can be done to help.
- awareness of group dynamics and the part they play in activities such as fellowship groups, Bible studies, church meetings and healing ministries.
- healing services could perhaps be restructured so as to minimize the potential for peer-pressure dissociation and so as to allow the Holy Spirit's true work to be seen for what it is.

- likewise, attempts at exorcism should not take place until the person has been assessed by a sympathetic psychiatrist.

Although, as I have said, psychiatry and religion have different methodologies and different languages, that does not, of course, stop us using both systems, both languages, simultaneously in order to try and arrive at some sort of satisfactory explanation for what might be going on in a particular patient. The model is no longer 'either/or' but a 'both/and' one.

There has been a growing realization in recent years, amongst psychiatrists, that the baby was thrown out with the bath-water when psychiatry betook itself to the high ground of scientific reductionism. Patients – who know better about these things – far from being overjoyed by the apparent triumph of science were profoundly dissatisfied by purely medical/chemical explanations for their suffering. Most patients want to understand their suffering, to personalize it and give it cosmic significance. To the victim, suffering has to have meaning, to be personalized, otherwise they feel invalidated as a human being. This is why the concentration camps were so terrible. One sees this striving after meaning in those who are bereaved and who say things like 'why did it happen to me?' 'What did I do to deserve this?'. When no obvious explanation comes to hand people reach outside of themselves for satisfaction. Humans are instinctively religious and religious metaphor constantly thrusts itself into conciousness when dealing with the sick and troubled.

Mental health professionals have a duty to respond to these inquiries and, if not perhaps qualified to answer them themselves, at least be able to arrange a meeting with someone who can. Explanations and meaning give power and control to those who feel threatened, helpless and out of control. In such circumstances religious explanations, rather than sociological, behavioural or medical explanations, often prove more satisfying. Psychoanalysts might remark that such beliefs are neurotic because when in distress threatened people regress to child-like ways of thinking. Religious solutions to suffering, they claim, reflect the re-emergence of animistic and self-centred views of the world which belong to immaturity. The Freudian analyst elaborates this further by maintaining that belief in God itself represents a persistence of childhood fantasies towards one's parents. However, for this hypothesis to prove acceptable one needs to demonstrate that religious people are immature and more likely to use other child-like patterns of thinking than their non-religious counterparts. Yet numerous sociological studies reveal that the reverse is true.[5] These show that religious people have lower rates of mental illness, tolerate stress and suffering with greater equanimity, and are better adjusted socially, occupationally and maritally than non-believers. Thus regression is not a sufficient explanation for religious belief or religious statements. Nonetheless, the psychoanalytic hypothesis is not entirely invalid. The kind of beliefs we adopt or the emphases we place upon them are not unrelated to our level of maturity and a child's faith is not the same as an adult's. Some religious beliefs, particularly those belonging to occult activities, can be seen as regressive or immature because of their self-centredness and preoccupation with power and control. In such circumstances well-judged psychotherapy can help the person to achieve a more mature *religious faith* as well as relief of symptoms and a more balanced outlook on life.

Addiction – A Model

Psychiatry, too, has much to gain from participation with religion. One area of particular interest to me is the biblical concept of possession, which recognizes that certain kinds of behaviour do have spiritual consequences and do have destructive potential for the person. This permits us to formulate a biblically-derived model of addiction and perhaps explains why it is that *religious* agencies have been particularly successful in helping patients to recover from various addictions such as to drugs and alcohol.

There are in fact *many* behaviours to which people appear to become increasingly addicted apart from drug and alcohol abuse: one thinks of gambling, violence, pornography, sexual perversions, and a variety of self-harming behaviours. The basis for addictive behaviour is the ancient biblically-derived principle that 'WE BECOME WHAT WE DO'.[6] It used to be believed that people acquired the facial features they had because of the way they consistently behaved. I am not sure that this is necessarily true but it does appear to be true of certain kinds of human behaviour and their effect upon the *inner* face – the personality. A degradation of the personality and decline in moral standards is a marked feature of the severely addicted drug addict. But this principle also seems to apply to more mundane situations:

- the materialist eventually becomes materialistic and finds it difficult to respect or value other people who are in menial, low-paid positions.
- the pornographer is so taken up with his fantasy life that he has difficulty in treating women as other than potential sex objects.
- the repeatedly violent man eventually loses the capacity to be vulnerable, to trust and to love other people.

This principle was well-understood by the Bible writers. It is found in Proverbs and St Paul gives a detailed and harrowing account in Romans 1 of what happens to men and women who reject God and surrender themselves to immorality. Jesus gave this model a specifically spiritual gloss when he told the Pharisees that it was not what went into a man that defiled him but what came out of him, 'For from within, out of men's hearts, come evil thoughts, sexual immorality, theft, murder, adultery, greed, malice, deceit, lewdness, envy, slander, arrogance and folly. All these evils come from inside and make a man unclean' (Mark 7.20). It is interesting to note that his list of vices corresponds to those behaviours now recognized as having an addictive or compulsive potential in the psychiatric sphere.

St Paul was obviously well aware of the destructive potential to the personality and spirit of those who indulge in morally damaging behaviour as shown by his careful use of the terminology 'debased' and 'degraded' in Romans 1. One sees this classically in the heroin addict who neglects himself, turns to crime, becomes totally self-centred, who lies both to himself and others, who becomes incapable of relationships with others, who eventually becomes a shell of his former self. This change in personality often proves the most upsetting aspect for the patient's family who no longer recognize the little boy they reared and once loved. Secondly, despite this self-destruction, the victim of an addiction nonetheless feels compelled to increase the extent of their behaviour. In all cases of addiction it is easier to deepen the addiction than to resist it.

Although one can invoke learning behaviour, it is an insufficient explanation for behaviour which is so obviously damaging to the biological system. There is no biological or sociological advantage to such addictions. Religious explanations which invoke a direct negative spiritual effect of such behaviour or even the influence of an external malignant spiritual agency not only satisfy emotionally but also fit the facts since religious conversion is still the most effective means of freeing someone from a major addiction. For the most powerful and sinister addictions the concept of possession also becomes an entirely appropriate model. Such surrender of the will does not happen overnight. There is a gradation of immersion in the chosen behaviour each step of which is marked by a further loss of self-determination and will and a further surrender to the behaviour itself.

This enables me to propose to you a model of addiction which satisfies both from the psychiatric and religious point of view. What starts out as an interest soon becomes a hobby, then an obsession, then a preoccupation, then an addiction and lastly a state of possession.

The biblical model of addictive behaviour

Interest $\longrightarrow$ Hobby $\longrightarrow$ Obsession $\longrightarrow$ Preoccupation $\longrightarrow$ Addiction/oppression $\longrightarrow$ Possession.

One can stop or be rescued at any point on this sliding scale although all successful treatment depends on a complete rejection of all addiction-related behaviour and its replacement with a new set of norms, behaviours and social contacts.

Addiction is only one relatively small facet of psychiatric work but I have used this as a model to show how specifically religious insights can enhance understanding and treatment from a psychiatric perspective. As a somewhat lighthearted exercise I have constructed an A–Z of disorders and situations which seem to me to share a psychiatric and spiritual component and in which some sort of joint cooperation between psychiatric and spiritual pastoral care might be particularly advantageous.

An A–Z of shared psychiatric/spiritual pathology

Addictions
Bereavement
Child abuse
Depression
Existential anxiety

Failure to forgive
Guilt
Hatred and anger
Idolatry (co-dependency in relationships)
Jealousy
Kleptomania and other recurrent crimes
Life crises
Marital conflict
Neuroses
Occultism
Psychopathy
Querulousness (abnormal illness-behaviour/hypochondriasis)
Rebelliousness and conduct disorders
Sexual perversions
Termination of pregnancy
Unbelief
Video-nasties
Women/men role issues
Xtraordinary psychological phenomena
Youth and the effects of certain child-rearing practices
Zealous overspiritualization

Conclusion

There is still a major gulf between psychiatric and religious professionals in the way they work and approach their patients even though there may be considerable overlap between them in terms of the people they are ministering to. Organizations such as the Association of Christian Psychiatrists aim to try and bridge that gulf through regular conferences, working with local clergy, writing and research and individuals' efforts to blend spiritual insights with clinical psychiatry and psychotherapy. There are now many organizations working in the hinterland between religion and psychiatry. If they are to make the fullest possible impact they need to be aware of each other's activities so that they can complement each other and avoid reproducing the same services. There is need for some central coordinating body which can identify areas of success, pool learned insights and publish research.

On the other hand, a lot of positive progress is being made in the relationship between psychiatry and religion. But, as always, God leaves us, as stewards of his creation, to use our intellects to make good what is deficient and to promote his purposes which are, in this context, healing and wholeness. In all instances of suffering there is a role for the expression of caring love, which is the hallmark of Christian maturity. Caring love also brings God directly into the situation and creates opportunities for other spiritual activities such as forgiveness, salvation or miraculous healing. Although I am not in a position to quantify this statement, I have observed over the years that Christian patients who enter prayerfully into their own psychiatric treatment enjoy accelerated rates of recovery. There is opportunity for a greater degree of cooperation than now exists between hospital chaplains, or other pastoral workers, and psychiatrists in the joint management of patients with mental disorders. Sadly, the therapeutic opportunities of such working together are sometimes marred by the spiritual confusion, unbelief and lack of confidence within the hospital chaplain. There is need for some chaplains to rediscover the power and simplicity of the gospel and for theological training colleges to ensure that the central tenets of the Christian faith are properly understood and put into practice. Psychiatrists, too, have a role to play in encouraging hospital chaplains and other pastoral care workers to be confident in putting these skills and insights into practice.

Psychiatry and Religion: A Response

Dr Blacker's paper has raised many significant points. Most significant was the fact that both religion and psychiatry have developed along different lines and because of this they may tend to focus on the difficulties in each field, rather than on what one field could do to complement what the other is doing in providing a wholeness to an approach to suffering. The lack of *working* contact between the two professions means that each has the feeling that they can cover most things without need for consultation with the other. This makes the ground ripe for projection, where the excesses of the other profession tend to be noted and a tug of war results as to which should chalk up the victory.

The Need for a Common Language

Perhaps what is necessary to offset the splitting apart is the development of a common language which grows out of working together. Let me illustrate what I mean. When I was in seminary in Cambridge, Massachusetts, the course in Medical Ethics was taught in conjunction with the Medical School at Harvard. The course was so popular that it was necessary to sign up for it a year in advance. We focused on cases which had been brought in by the students or sent in previous years. The notes on the cases were photocopied so that each student had them. Discussion was lively because it centred around true-life events. The medical students were able to tell about the course of particular diseases which were referred to and the theological students were able to fill the medical students in on the steps for making ethical choices from what they had learned in Moral Theology. This did several things:

1. It trained the students to be able to explain simply, without a lot of jargon, the information the others needed to know; because it was a mixed professional group one had to 'translate' jargon and find a common language in which to talk.

2. Practice in working together professionally was built into the training. I had not realized what an impact this had until later, when as a hospital chaplain I would go in quite comfortably to ward rounds on the perhaps mistaken assumption that everyone had been trained in the same fashion that I was. It came as a shock when I found that this was not so.

3. There seemed to be something in the synthesis of the two disciplines speaking together which came out with a more whole approach to whatever was being discussed. I also noted that after a time, the more I tended to ask 'medical questions', the more the medics delighted in telling me that I was on the 'wrong track', that it really was an existential problem.

The common language which seemed to evolve from such discussions was a story-telling mode supplemented by scientific thinking. Let me explain.

I worked for a while in a multi-disciplinary team doing psycho-therapy. There was the usual input which was necessary about the psychiatric condition and the medication which was being given. Because the group was analytically oriented, we began to notice that the patients' progress was in large part related to the way they were described by the therapist. If the therapist said, 'Mrs Jones is paranoid', there was a knowing shake of heads all around with a feeling that there was not much that could be done. If the therapist said, 'Mrs Jones is afraid a lot of the time' then she seemed to be treated as a person by the team and the therapist and made some progress. We therefore agreed collectively to use as little psychiatric naming as possible and keep in the 'story-telling' mode. We could then begin to talk about Mrs Jones' beliefs, which not only included her fears that she was being followed, but also what she hoped and desired for herself. What it was important for her to do in life. Now, of course, we were talking theology, but without embarrassment because there was no jargon. In this way, the psychiatric, the existential, and the theological were put in terms that everyone could understand. We had a common language.

Several times, the unit on which we worked had someone come in who wanted to see a Christian therapist. At first we would try to accommodate the request, but without challenging the person's reasons very much. On one occasion when there was not anyone available who was in that category, we decided to handle it in a different way. The person was asked to state what they believed was important and to clarify what was centrally important to them that they *did not want changed or challenged*. When it was agreed that this would be respected and the therapist would not make interpretations in this area, this was acceptable to the person. We then discussed as a team what similar areas in our own lives which were sacred to us that we would not want a therapist to interpret away. In this way our central beliefs were acknowledged to each other. Again, this was done in a common language rather than switching into theological jargon, which was important. There is another important principle which came out of this. That is, implicit religion.

Implicit Religion

An approach that can be used in both psychiatry and theology is the analysis of where a person is in terms of their beliefs. In medicine, when a person goes into hospital the first task is to find out where a person *is* and then work from there to where they may want to be. It is possible to do this in spiritual matters. That is, to establish where a person's beliefs lie in relation to their actions. This can be reflected back to see if this is where the person wants to be. How does this work?

Paul Tillich says that one's religion is one's 'ultimate concern'. On this basis it is possible to see what the person's implicit religion is in terms of their actions. These may also serve as examples as to how spiritual issues can be handled on a practical level. Let me give a few examples.

1. A man came into a counselling session sobbing. I asked him what was wrong. He said that his son was going to school for the first time. Puzzled as to why this should provoke such a reaction, I asked him to say more. He said that he had been so caught up in his work that he had never once been able to get home before the child went to bed to read him a bed-time story. Each day he had tried but failed. He realized that he had missed his son's entire childhood. After exploring things on a psychological level, I reflected that on the surface he had felt that his family was the most important thing in the world (his 'ultimate concern'), however, in practice, his real 'religion' was his work. On the altar of this religion he had sacrificed being able to spend time with his son. This was where he was at. He could either confirm his present religious arrangement by carrying on as he was doing, or would have to make sacrifices in his current 'religion' in order to spend more time at home.

2. Students from theological colleges used to come to the psychiatric hospital where I worked for Applied Pastoral Theology. During this time they would be in small groups to look at the way God was working within and through them to each other. On one occasion, one student said that he did not 'believe' in this sort of exercise, that he felt that a priest should be 'above' the conflicts of life and the expression of feelings, and that people expected this of a priest. I suggested that he was saying that he did not believe in the incarnation (where God got involved in our 'mess' in Jesus). I asked whether in fact he really did not believe in the incarnation, or whether he was perhaps afraid of involvement and was dressing up his fear as a belief.

3. While administering Communion at hospital one Sunday I came to a woman kneeling at the altar rail. She shouted out, 'I am not worthy', and collapsed sobbing over the rail. Immediately the woman kneeling next to her said, 'In that case, have a polo mint my dear', and offered her some. The woman seemed startled. I said that if she did not feel ready to receive the sacrament, she was free to receive the polo mint. After careful thought, she said, 'I think I'll stick with polo mint today'. I said, 'Fine', gave her a blessing, and went on down the rail. Next Sunday she was back. As I began to administer Communion she leaned over past everyone else and

said, 'Worthy this week, Father'. Everyone cheered. After the administration, I told the congregation that I thought something significant had happened just then. Just as when we are ill, we can only eat broth, so she was only able to eat the 'broth' of a polo mint last week, which a fellow sufferer had given her. That act of kindness had strengthened her to be able to receive the 'real thing' this week. The sacramental act had led her to the sacrament, and that was in the gift of each of us to do for each other.

This, then, is how to uncover implicit religion – to deduce belief from action, reflect it back and ask the person if that is in fact what they believe. If they do believe it, the next step is to ask if that is what they wish to continue to believe, and leave them to make up their minds about change. Basically, until we know where we are, we do not know what changes are needed to get somewhere else.

I once got lost while driving in London. I stopped the car, looked at the London A to Z map, put my finger on where I wanted to go on the map and drove off again. Almost immediately I stopped, laughing. It was no good knowing where I wanted to go unless I knew where I was. So, I got out, looked at the street signs, found where I was on the map, then looked at what changes I had to make to arrive at my destination.

Most people have belief systems of which they are not fully aware. In its root, religion comes from 're-ligio' that to which the person is tied down. Implicit religion may be different from expressed faith. It is the central thing which, when it goes, leaves us in a crisis of faith as to whether or not to go on.

There is implicit religion in the beliefs surrounding medicine itself. For instance, one often hears faith statements directed towards medicine. 'I *believe* that some day medical science will be able to cure the disease which is killing me.' When pressed further, that belief might even state: 'If all the diseases were thus cured, then medical science will be able to cure death.' Hence, immortality in this life would be possible if we take enough exercise and get to the doctor soon enough. While we can 'see through' this on a logical level, the assumptions are nevertheless there, resulting in embarrassment or a feeling of 'what went wrong' when death occurs. This implicit belief system is perhaps more apparent in America where, whenever death occurs, thought is given to what the doctor might have done wrong. This belief system seems to be held simultaneously with Christian belief in the resurrection. To bring these two beliefs to a point of dialogue with each other is a task which, in some way, parallels looking at the belief systems of religion and psychiatry on a professional working basis. We are often not aware that we may carry within us several religions, some incompatible. I am aware of this myself. Even though I am a priest who believes in the Christian faith, I still don't walk under ladders. It's bad luck! Where does that belief come from? Not recognizing that in myself, I might split that off to challenge others who are not 'pure believers'. The dialogue between psychiatry and religion is also something which marks the split of multiple belief systems within ourselves. To identify and understand these is important. It is also important which of these is the 'dominant' one.

Healthy Religion

Dr Blacker makes the point that psychiatry sees the distortions of religion without seeing religious faith 'in its healthy normative mode'. What is the normative healthy mode of religion? This is a challenging question. Dr Michael Wilson has a useful phrase that 'illness is when the part takes over the whole'.[7] For me, this is a useful concept in looking at the normative religious mode. Idolatry is when a 'good' takes over the whole and becomes an end in itself. Theology is a balance of seemingly opposite extremes: transcendence/immanence, judgement/forgiveness, church gathered/church scattered. These should be held in balance. Spiritual illness comes when some aspect of these takes over the other, for example, when someone preaches or feels judged as if there is no such thing as forgiveness; or forgives all and sundry as if there is no such thing as judgement.

People tend to take religious beliefs and use them to carpet over the distortions in their personalities, either collectively or individually. For some, religion consists of a 'holy war' against unbelievers to the exclusion of all else. At given times, groups and cultures in their collective belief have the same illness. The question that needs to be raised is 'Why at this particular time does this part of religion take over the rest?' If work is done on an illness within an individual in the personality, it is also necessary to work with the distortions in the belief system on a theological level or else the corresponding theological distortions will cause the person to feel guilty about changes or to cling to former ways of thinking. Worse, they may ascribe their former beliefs to the religion and leave the religion altogether. It seems quite central to look at what is the part that takes over the whole, not only in terms of the people we are trying to help, but our own professions as well. Here others can help us see what we may be blind to.

With regard to seeing the distortions, I would coin the term 'impertise'. Experts 'know more and more about less and less', and their opposites might be called 'imperts' (from 'impertinent'), and are much like the child in the story of the 'Emperor's New Clothes' who shouted out in the crowd as the emperor rode by in his imaginary finery: 'Mummy, why is the king only wearing his underwear?'. This is, in fact, the prophetic function which the disciplines of psychiatry and religion can also do for one another. It keeps the distortions (illnesses) down when the semi-important threatens to take over. It is, of course, what the therapist does for his or her patient as well, as the illness is wrestled with in order to be put in its place, from trying to take possession of the whole to being understood as part.

Diagnosis and Discernment

Another question which I think was raised by Dr Blacker is, how do we develop the expertise of working in the spiritual field? Part of my work is being a Continuing Ministerial Education Officer for the Diocese of Oxford, and I am aware at the moment of the number of people interested in spiritual direction. This is a field which is not like psychotherapy, but which tries to help the person with theological skills to be able to discern what is happening on a spiritual level in the person's life. It uses primarily discernment (which is more on an intuitive level) rather than diagnosis (which is on a thinking level). It seeks to help people discern what God is doing in their lives and to enable them to help others.

To appreciate the distinction between diagnosis and discernment we need to look more closely at the differences between psychiatry and theology. While they do need to develop a common language, the fact is that they are different disciplines looking at things from different perspectives, and so have different means of arriving at the different forms of reality which they are each seeking. Vicktor Frankl says that there are different dimensions of explanation.[8] You can look at the same phenomenon from different disciplines and they could be right on different levels. For instance, consider the story of Romeo and Juliet: on the physical level, it can be described as being an example of the effect of hormones acting in young people's lives. A psychologist could see it as a case of adolescent identity formation by the young people rebelling against their parents' wishes. A theologian might see it as the story of how two innocent deaths reconcile two warring families.

Each would be right according to the discipline concerned. None would be completely right. Romeo and Juliet may be a case of hormone action, but the story is not *just* about hormones. To say that it is leaves out all the other levels.

In psychiatry, the collective 'rule book' is the *Diagnostic and Statistical Manual of Mental Disorders*, abbreviated DSM-III-R. In this book, under each mental disorder, there is listed a set of symptoms, some or all of which have to be present in order to have the disease. This is a diagnostic approach – rationally analytical. It is a 'road map' which is necessary to treat someone on a medical level.

Would such an approach be appropriate to see if someone had a vocation to pastoral ministry? Probably not. Vocation is on the spiritual level, and one would look to discern, rather than diagnose. Patterns would be looked for, but a feeling about whether or not it was leading one into that ministry would use a different form of arriving at the truth, based on prayerful attention to what is happening. Both theology and psychiatry use diagnosis *and* discernment, but the primary tools of each is different, and calls for a different set of skills. Psychiatry needs to use clearly and carefully designed categories; theology looks at the leading of the Spirit, and expresses itself in more symbolic modes.

To make the point, I want you to imagine sitting across a candle-lit dining table with the person you love.. You take their hand in yours, look deeply into their eyes, and say, 'Although you are composed of 95 per cent water plus a few trace elements, yet the clusters of your molecules are put together in a not unpleasing form. One recognizes that one's hormonal activity rises in direct proportion to one's physical proximity to yourself. One desires to mix one's genes for the production of subsequent progeny. In order to expedite this would you give me your response within thirty days, or more quickly if possible.'

Isn't that moving! Factually and diagnostically it is correct. Yet it is humorous because it is using an inappropriate, though accurate, mode of description. Beliefs and things of ultimate importance would use language of discernment and metaphor: 'I have noticed increasingly how very much you mean to me. I love you, and want you to share my life and what I have, to be a companion on my journey, to wear each other's rings, and to be joined as one'. Not very scientific-sounding!

While it is of psychological interest to know that religious people recover more quickly from psychological illness, that information is not helpful for one to 'make sense on the cosmic level' of what is happening to them in their suffering. This requires a 'story-telling, metaphorical and mythical mode' and one in which there is discernment ('gut-level' recognition) rather than head-level diagnosis. The story-telling level is a different, though complementary, level to the exploration of psychiatry and should not be confused or amalgamated into a single mode.

There would seem to be a possibility for useful cooperation and consultation between psychiatrists and spiritual directors. Some excellent work has been done in this field by Gerald May, who is both a psychiatrist and a spiritual director. His book *Care of Mind, Care of Spirit* is one of the most important and useful books I have read.[9] It distinguishes carefully, but concisely, between depression and 'dark night of the soul' experiences. His book *Addiction and Grace* explores the area of religious belief and addiction.[10] Both books are written in a readable way but with the fine tuning of a discernment which can distinguish between two things which seem very alike but are not. While psychiatrists should work with parish priests, I think it is also necessary to say that parish clergy may not have the training for the specialized work which the spiritual director might have in particularly sensitive cases.

Sacramental Aspects of Medicine

Another area which I think religion and psychiatry might usefully work on together is the idea of the sacramental in ordinary life.

After an occasion in which I was called to be present at the death of a distressed person in hospital, there was a discussion with the staff of the unit on how they might be of help in a sacramental way when a person is dying. The person whom I was called to see was a patient in a psychiatric hospital who had been unable to talk for years, yet was in distress. As she could hear, I used a guided meditation and the sense of touch to help her focus on what was troubling her, then to give it into the hands of God, receive forgiveness, and meet her death in a less troubled way. In the discussion of how the nurses might be able to do the same thing, the idea came up of a sacramental blanket bath. They felt that if they gave a bath as if the person was the most valued and important person in the world that they could communicate to each of the patients what I had tried to do with the dying woman. They also looked at the way in which they handed out medication. In handing out medication in the same way the chaplain handed out communion: 'Here is something which we are giving you which we feel will help you' with touch and warmth, medication then became sacramental of care rather than 'doctor's orders'.

When I visited the ward after the seminar, two nurses were giving blanket baths to Beethoven's Pastoral Symphony while others were taking care and attention over the medication to express the same Holy Caring. This reflection of the spiritual importance of ordinary work in medicine is of central importance, so that the spiritual activities are not relegated to the chaplain alone, but are done by everyone present. This then opened the door to the staff being able to share with one another why they entered nursing and medicine as a vocation. This is particularly important at the moment where the norm is swinging to a market economy and away from the vocational aspects, which is causing spiritual damage to those who have entered psychiatry as a vocation. Recently our Department of Psychotherapy have had an academic term of spirituality and psychiatry to explore this dimension.

The Chaplain, the Psychiatrist and the Problem of Evil

I want to grasp the nettle here and look at the problem of evil, and the way the medical profession and the Christian may come at it from different perspectives. This may help us see how the chaplain and psychiatrist differ, and where they can come together.

Let us first look at the problem of evil. The one thing which Christians of every denomination agree on is the centrality of the

Lord's Prayer. It is Jesus' prayer, which he taught his disciples; it is his own words. He says, 'Lead us not into temptation, but deliver us from evil'. Presumably there would be no need to put in the supplication asking God not to lead us into temptation unless there were a danger of him doing so. There is, because he has. The story of Job is one example where God comes to an arrangement with the Satan to tempt Job. They form a partnership with each other through their wager about whether or not Job can be tempted into sin. The Satan is part of God's creation and he is using him.

A second incident of this kind is Jesus' temptation in the wilderness. 'Then Jesus *was led by the Spirit* out into the wilderness *to be tempted by the devil*' (Matthew 4.1). In short, Jesus meets the devil, not through the wiles of the devil, but because God, acting through the Spirit, introduces them to each other for a purpose. Why?

Last autumn, in order to avoid catching influenza I went for an inoculation. The nurse, a friend of mine who wanted to help me, injected into me a strain of the very flu which I was afraid of getting. She led my body into 'temptation' (in terms of catching the flu) and I thanked her for it. In being introduced to, and fighting, temptation I did not catch flu. More accurately, the flu may have come, but it did not possess me by taking me over. My body had been prepared and strengthened to fight it.

Let us look at how the process of temptation which Jesus experienced in the wilderness helped him. Jesus in fact did everything the devil tempted him to do, *but in a different way and for different reasons.*

- The devil tempted him to turn stones into bread to feed himself and satisfy his own needs. Jesus picks up this theme, but changes ordinary bread into eternal bread to feed others.
- He was tempted to throw himself off the temple (to risk destroying his own body to amaze the multitudes). Jesus picks up the theme, he offers his body for destruction on the cross (again publicly) which leads to the resurrection (transformation rather than rescue).
- the devil tempts Jesus to worship him and so gain all the kingdoms of the world. Jesus takes up this theme, worships God, and now is worshipped by some in every country of the world.

The process here is accepting the evil that is presented and *transforming* it into something more constructive, caring and eternal.

So, while the psychiatrist and chaplain both offer counselling, it is not the same thing. The psychiatric form of counselling is to face and accept what has happened to one, alleviate the suffering where possible, and act appropriately and realistically in one's changed circumstances.

Evil as such should always be resisted. It is destructive in that it can take over. The chaplain's job is to assist those who suffer to use it as an occasion of transformation. It is in this respect that evil never has the last word. The chaplain starts at the level of trying to change things for the better, but his or her primary aim is towards transformation. Taking the same ingredients and reforming them so that God can use them in their resurrected form for something useful and loving for others in an eternal sense.

An example of this is someone whom I was counselling who planned a well-prepared suicide attempt which 'failed'. It failed in that the means of suicide had broken. We explored whether this was 'coincidence' or 'miracle'. If it were miracle, then his happiness was of secondary importance. God had saved him for a purpose. That person now helps people whom others have usually given up. This was on the level of transformation – spiritual rather than 'let's see if you can reorder your life to live less destructively' – which would be the purely psychological approach.

God at Work?

It seems, in looking through Scripture, that God makes his opportunities through need. Therefore, in looking at what God might be doing, we might look at need and see what is happening.

As the health service in the UK goes to a market economy, the vocational aspect of work is neglected. This makes it all the more important to look at it. As violence and drugs take over the fabric of society, it makes it more of a necessity for the theological perspective to combine with the skills of psychiatry to meet that need. The list which Dr Blacker has added at the end of his paper correctly summarizes the outstanding need.

Paradoxically, it may be that the emphasis on the 'market' approach is a 'necessary evil' which is there to transform chaplaincy work. The health service managers have pointed out that chaplains may not be hired unless they are 'useful' (whatever that means). This challenges chaplains to sharpen up their theological skills and prove their usefulness in a cost-conscious health service, which may be no bad thing, both for the health service and for the chaplaincy.

In the same way, the patients (now called 'users') are more readily listened to by the managers if they say 'not good enough' than they were when treated as less than a full person with spiritual needs as well as physical and mental ones.

What I have found is that, by working on a team with other professionals, and putting forward things on a psychological level (which is part of my level of expertise), when I contribute the spiritual dimension, it is listened to. By listened to, I do not mean fully accepted. I mean first tolerated as irrelevant, heard with amusement (there he goes again), and finally heard with respect. It means going around all the wards as chaplain, but making a firm commitment to work with one or two teams as an integral member of the team. It is this involvement (incarnation) with a team on a work-a-day basis where it all happens, and this informs the rest of the work, and sharpens up the skills of theological reflection.

I think that the dialogue between the two disciplines, which ranges from respect to 'what do you think you are playing at', is a love-hate relationship which will bear fruit. Maybe the psychiatric profession and the theological profession are far enough apart now to have established separate identities and not to be threatened by one another. There real dialogue can begin. Maybe this too is the work of God. We will work together more closely when we discover, through the grace of God, that we can no longer afford to be able to go it alone in our separate disciplines.

References

1. E.M. Pattison, 'Ideological Support for the Marginal Middle Class: Faith Healing and Glossolalia', in I.I. Zaretsky and M.P. Leone (eds.), *Religious Movement in Contemporary America* (Princeton University Press 1974).
2. D. Hambidge, 'Survey of Cross-Training in Psychiatry and Religious Belief (1993)', an unpublished paper presented at the Royal College of Psychiatrists Conference, Scarborough, 1993. For copies please write to: Dr D. Hambidge, New Life Christian Fellowship, Newland, Lincoln LN1 1XG, UK.

3. D.B. Larson, M.E. Paterson, D.G. Blazer, 'Systematic Analysis of Research on Religious Variables in Four Major Psychiatric Journals (1978–1982)', *American Journal of Psychiatry* 143 (1986), 329–334.

4. K.A. Sherrill and D.B. Larson, 'The Systematic Review: A Brief Overview', Proceedings of the Paul Tournier Institute Conference on the Christian Doctor, November 6–10, 1991.

5. D. Larson, 'Holy Health', *Christianity Today*, Nov. 1992.

6. For example, Psalm 115.8; Proverbs 13.20.

7. M. Wilson, *Hospital as a Place of Truth* (University of Birmingham Institute for the Study of Worship and Religious Architecture 1971).

8. V. Frankl, *The Will to Meaning* (Souvenir Press 1971).

9. G. May, *Care of Mind, Care of Spirit* (Harper & Row 1982)

10. G. May, *Addiction and Grace* (Harper & Row 1988).

Useful Addresses

The Association for the Pastoral Care of the Mentally Ill, 39 St John's Lance, London EC1M 4BJ.

The Association of Christian Psychiatrists. Secretary: Dr C.V.R. Blacker; Gwaynten Unit, Royal Cornwall Hospital Truro, Cornwall.

Christians in Caring Professions (CiCP), Kings' House, 175 Wokingham Road, Reading, Berks RG6 1LT.

Christian Action Research and Education (CARE), 53 Romney Street, London SW1P 3RF.

The Church's Council for Health and Healing, St Marylebone Road Parish Church, Marylebone Road, London NW1 5LT.

CHAPTER 7

Growing Old and Dying

—

Dr Ann Bradshaw
Revd Leonard Lunn

St Paul calls death 'the last enemy' (1 Corinthians 15.26). For those involved in healing ministry, the death of the person being cared for often seems like a great defeat. Yet we must all die (Hebrews 9.27). Christians involved in healing ministry must, therefore, have a theology which encompasses death. For most people death comes only after they have grown old, experiencing various kinds of weakness and impairment. This, too, must be taken account of in our theology. These issues are the subject of the following chapter, which is written by a nurse who lectures in palliative care and a hospice chaplain.

> But man – we, scaffold of score brittle bones;
> who breathe from groundlong babyhood to hoary
> age gasp; whose breath is our momento mori . . .'
> Gerard Manley Hopkins[1]

Daily I am growing older, and one day I will die. That is the truth for each of us. The material processes of daily living bring with them the sure and certain knowledge that our bodies are gradually decaying and eventually will cease to function. As we grow older we are faced with our own ageing and the prospect of death. But while the process of growing old necessarily brings with it the inevitability of dying, it does not follow that dying is always a result of growing old. Death is capricious, each of us may be confronted by death and dying at any stage of our lives.

Nevertheless, the clarity of this truth is now obscured for most of people in the west. Unlike previous centuries, and indeed other cultures, death is not a daily, visible, normal and expected part of our lives. We repress the expectation of death for ourselves and those whom we love. And because of advances in medical science, many more of us continue, and can expect to continue, to survive into old age, and indeed, into an old age that for many will mean being older and fitter and more comfortable than was so for any previous generation.

But while these processes of ageing may take longer as our lifespan increases, nevertheless, they merely postpone the final confrontation with the loss of our lives. For, in both the process of growing old and the final state of dying, loss is the common theme. In growing old we gradually lose our physical strength, our mental capability, our social status and often our financial security, and sometimes, as they too grow and die, those whom we love. In dying we lose life itself.

Two of the most popular television comedies of recent years in Britain have been 'Waiting for God' and 'One Foot in the Grave'. Both of these programmes attracted audiences of several million, the titles speaking volumes about their subjects of ageing and dying. This may mean that the final taboo is broken, or simply that we are at least ready to laugh at ourselves in the ultimate and inevitable predicament. And yet, the constant state of protest which defines the central characters suggests an underlying realism that is rarely confronted. Perhaps, as T.S. Eliot writes, 'Human kind cannot bear very much reality.'

And indeed, Alex Comfort's experience of working as a physician to the elderly makes him impatient of those who philosophize about the beauty of old age. Old age is a time of loss, not ripening, of decaying and diminishing. 'Ageing is impairment; it is the progressive dissolution of what we have built up throughout our lives . . . One goes around the wards and one realizes that these women were once beautiful, or at least young; these men were once people and we no longer treat them as people'.[2] We may be reminded of the now famous poem, Kate, part of nursing folklore.[3] It is said to have been left on a hospital locker, written by an old woman, Kate, who longs for the nurses to see beyond her slow, irritatingly useless body into the reality of her youthful and loving self within:

> . . . I'm an old woman now
> and nature is cruel,
> 'Tis her jest to make

171

old age look a fool.
The body it crumbles,
grace and vigour depart,
There now is a stone
Where once I had a heart:
But inside this old carcase
a young woman still dwells . . .
So open your eyes nurses,
Open and see,
Not a crabbit old woman,
look closer – see ME.

From a materialistic perspective, then, the path we take as we grow old and die is merely the disintegration of atoms and molecules, nerves and tissues. 'Sans teeth, sans eyes, sans taste, sans everything' (*As You Like It*, II, vii). And, in that case, like Nietzsche we may want to question whether we want to take that path at all: 'To die proudly when it is no longer possible to live proudly. Death of one's own free choice, death at the proper time, with a clear head and with joyfulness . . . '.[4]

James Casson, a young General Practitioner, has written movingly of his personal experience of dying from cancer:

Dying makes life suddenly real. Watching my slow physical deterioration reaffirmed my belief that there is something else within, which would survive if only because my personality stayed the same in spite of the eroding bodily form in which it is confined. Slowly I have come to terms with my own circumstances, though each must find his own way to resolve the conflict.[5]

And perhaps both Kate and James Casson raise the key question for us. As I go through my own changing life, as I move from my babyhood, through my childhood, my youth, my middle age, and eventually to being old, who am I? What is the *real* me?

The Nature of the Human Being

For the materialist the human being, the real me, is nothing more than a heap of chemicals which are gradually deteriorating and decomposing over time. All we can do as human beings is to try and use medical and scientific knowledge and techniques to hold back the process, to prolong physical health and postpone the inevitable disintegration. For the existential philosopher the very knowledge of this process can be positive. My life is more than mere material processes, for it is my personal journey, focused and sharpened by confrontation with death, a journey of self-actualization, of discovering and becoming what I really am and what I really want to be. And indeed, we could not disagree with either of these perspectives. Yet we have to ask if this is all we are, in Simone Weil's words, are we ultimately nothing more than a 'little pile of inert matter'?[6] Does my personal journey end with me, on my own?

For those of us whose foundations lie in the beliefs and values of the Judeo-Christian tradition, life is a personal journey that is essentially a journey for relationship with our Creator and ultimately for the eternal destiny for which we are intended. From a theocentric perspective then, although the journey of growing old and dying is a personal journey for each one of us, no matter how lonely or isolated we may feel, the objective reality is that we are not alone. From a theological understanding, human beings are created in the image of God and human life is lived for relationship with God. So then, although our journey takes place in time and so marks the limits of our human existence, nevertheless, it is the life journey in which I prepare myself for my Creator with the assurance that my Creator walks with me. Here is the divergence between existential philosophy and orthodox theology. The purpose for which we were created in time, in material bodies that grow old and die, is to grow into relationship for life eternal, into a fulfilment in which our bodies will be transformed. This will be the fulfilment and culmination of the *real* me. 'So we do not lose heart. Though our outer nature is wasting away, our inner nature is being renewed every day' (2 Corinthians 4.16 RSV).

The popular view of the television characters, Victor and Diana, angry and defiant at a world that somehow belittles them, is turned upside down. For as we grow old and confront our dying we do not become merely people whose infirmity makes us decreasingly useful to society, a useless burden on our families and a drain on the state. Rather we are the people with the potential wisdom to grow closer to God and to light the way for others. The biblical tradition teaches that old age is the time of wisdom and maturity. Our bodies may grow weaker but we are of no less value to God.

So, although our ministry may change our practical involvement in the world ought not. Active practical service may gradually be replaced by the vital but unseen ministry of prayer and the imparting of wisdom learnt through life experience. Ageing is a time of learning and adapting, and in the Judeo–Christian tradition, a time of the development of personal and practical wisdom through our deepening knowledge of God. As the writer of Proverbs tells us: 'The glory of young men is their strength, but the beauty of old men is their grey hair' (Proverbs 20.29). And as Job declares: 'Wisdom is with the aged, and understanding in length of days' (Job 12.12).

Yet, ageing also means that we need to learn how to be dependent and to accept help. In our contemporary society, with families now often far apart, or even broken down, this help may need to be from strangers. This is not as it should be. The Ten Commandments are clear: 'Honour your father and your mother, as the Lord your God commanded you; that your days may be prolonged, and that it may go well with you, in the land which your Lord your God gives you' (Deuteronomy 5.16 RSV). We not only have a moral responsibility to our children, we also have a moral responsibility to honour our parents, and especially as they age and need us. And if the elderly are to share their wisdom with those of us who are still young, then we need to give time to listen to them, and we need to listen with respect. This is how we honour them.

Thus we see that our lives are the means of our developing as persons, as we each seek to live out our purposes. The incarnation of God in Christ is both our model and our hope. So then, the ultimate purpose and destiny of the lives of each one of us depends on the nature of the God who created us and the way he enters into his creation. On this rests our whole theology and so the basis not only for individual journeys, but also for our practical actions as we seek to cooperate with our Creator and respond to our fellow travellers.

God becoming a human being is the basis for our knowledge of God as love, a God who not only identifies with us, but is prepared for the same human life as us. He knows what it is to be born, to grow older, and to die. He knows the loneliness of suffering, the experience of abandonment, the feeling that he is separated even from God himself: 'My God, my God, why have you forsaken me?'

(Matthew 27.46). It is not overdramatizing to say that growing old and dying have these ingredients. As with Job, the problem of suffering – so often associated with growing old and dying – is concerned with the silence and apparent absence of God. So we feel he must share our powerlessness, or his victory seems hollow. It is in the scandal of the cross that we see God's identification and compassionate presence in the deepest human pain. We may not understand, but we know he cares because he is there. That surely is enough for our theology of God? In the aftermath of Auschwitz this is the God we need today, a God who identifies with our suffering. A God who suffers yet remains God. 'The bystander in the concentration camp at Auschwitz, suffering with no words to speak, was given words by the story of Jesus: "God is here, hanging there on the gallows".'[7]

The theologian Paul Fiddes argues that God in his transcendent omnipotence chooses to opt for love and is therefore voluntarily self-limited.[8] His almighty power makes this happen because he wishes it. God chooses to suffer not because he desires suffering, but because he desires fellowship with his creation. And because he chooses suffering he is not ruled by it. Suffering cannot overwhelm him. So by God's desire death and its attendant suffering continues to exist because the divine will has opted for love and freedom rather than supreme omnipotence. In effect this means that God is somehow bound, as we are, in a universe that has a randomness that makes death threatening and unbearable when, for example, it comes too soon to the young or too slowly to the afflicted elderly. So God develops in response to his creation. God is not impassable, changeless, perfect. He has limited himself because of his great love for us. He too is in time. He too suffers. And the mark of that suffering, God's own self-justification, is the cross.

But Frances Young, the theologian and mother of a severely handicapped child, is moved by her own experience to question this position. She writes:

As one who has written about God's suffering, I have to confess that there remains a niggling worry that God's changelessness and impassability remain important ideas. For how can a vulnerable God still be God, a God to worship and depend upon? If you are tempted to sigh 'Poor old God', what kind of a God are you left with?[9]

Frances Young appreciates that theologians such as Fiddes are wrestling with the important idea that, just as we are changed in our relationships, so God's love must also involve him in some kind of change if he is not merely to be 'an uninvolved do-gooder'.[10] Yet, she believes that even if we use human analogies, we need to be aware that we live with a tension. As human beings we are ambivalent about our feelings as giving depth to our relationships, but we also value peace of mind, serenity and order. And she believes that in order to function in a pastoral role, to be of use to those who suffer, we need to hold back from becoming too involved. Indeed, she illustrates her argument from a personal experience when she was involved with a couple whose daughter was stillborn. Her own deep involvement in their suffering made her realize that she was reliving her own pain. Her struggle meant that she was no use to the parents. Only when the self-involvement was purged could she begin to be of use to those who were suffering. And it was this personal experience of the strength of God which enables the sufferer to withstand suffering that caused her to write:

> From that experience I found myself reclaiming the insight that God is 'beyond suffering' in the sense that he is not emotionally involved in a self-concerned way – rather he is that ocean of love that can absorb all the suffering of the world and purge it without being polluted or changed by it. And yet at the same time in Christ he subjected himself to personal involvement in pain and anguish, so that in some sense he genuinely knows what it feels like to be victim and shares in our experience of suffering. The two ideas somehow belong together, and . . . our knowledge of God is impoverished if we cannot stretch our minds and imagination to encompass both.[11]

So here we have an understanding of God's suffering love, compassion, *agape*, holding within him both immanence and transcendence, subjectivity and objectivity, involvement and detachment. Compassion is a suffering love, but also an overcoming love, and thus a love that rules with justice and mercy. And of course the nature of God as love must involve justice. But justice involves judgement and judgement itself presupposes that the judge, while part of the system, must at the same time be separate from and indeed, transcend the system, if he is to be a truly impartial judge. And surely the greatest lesson of Auschwitz is not just the terrible spectre of suffering, as terrifyingly awful as this is, but most especially the wickedness and evil of human sin that not only made it possible, but turned a blind eye when it happened. And such hideousness is built into us all. This is all our responsibility. In our anguish over Auschwitz, and our desire to find a theology post-Auschwitz, a way of understanding where God is in such terrible suffering, are we putting God and not man in the dock? The people who perished in Auschwitz need more than passive compassion for they are owed the compassion of justice. The compassion and righteousness of love demand judgement for the terrors of human sin, a judgement of us all.

So, as Barth believes, death is the great reminder of creaturely mortality and the ultimate consequence of sin as separation from God. But Barth is definite in his assertion that this is the extent of human knowledge. 'Death, as it actually encounters us men, is the sign of God's judgement on us. We cannot say less than this, but of course we cannot say more than this either'.[12] Yet as death brings into clear focus God's revealed nature as a God of judgement, it also clearly reveals the grounding of that judgement in a God of love; for, as Barth himself says, God's law presupposes God's grace. This is the absolute message of both the crucifixion and the resurrection. For the message of the crucifixion is God's identification with the sins and suffering of humanity, groaning in the effects of the fall; but the message of the resurrection tells of the incomprehensible sovereignty of God and his promise that, in spite of everything, not all is irretrievably lost. In Christ, his death and resurrection, is our hope. So while we need to be careful not to move too quickly from Good Friday to Easter, to minimize the scandal of the cross, we need to remember that the victory, for us, is won.

Thus death is not just a welcome end to earthly misery and suffering, as in Buddhism, but through Christ's victory it is a sign of real transforming hope. The future hope for humans is actualized by God himself with the promise of eternal life. This is the real wholeness or salvation in which the human being is able to fulfil his or her true humanity and find peace. This means that healing and wholeness, the peace of salvation, is not just in the realms of the spiritual as if this is distinct from the material, but includes the material body. Thus human beings, in all aspects of their suffering, have a future hope of being made whole; the body, mind and relationships are to be healed and repaired as they respond to the offer of salvation. As Charley writes, *shalom*, the biblical idea of peace, is not merely the end of hostility or anger, but 'health, wholeness, harmony' through the covenant relationship with God.[13] The resurrection body holds within it the idea of newness and ultimate goodness, transfiguration into a new mode of practical existence.

Yet, on a personal level, when those we love die, the answers seem simplistic and trite, just too easy. Whatever our carefully thought out theology, in the pain of suffering we feel only the anger at the seeming injustice of it all. As for C.S. Lewis, the reality does not match the intellectual, our heart and our head are split asunder. His carefully thought out arguments in *The Problem of Pain* seemed of little help to him in his grief after the death of his wife.[14] As he remonstrates with the College Chaplain in the stage play, *Shadowlands*, who was offering traditional pastoral comfort, 'No! it will not do, it will not do.' The awful terror and misery and pain of suffering and death are only too real.

But as C.S. Lewis traces his grief in *A Grief Observed* through his feeling of isolation and rejection by God, his question as to whether God is a 'cosmic sadist',[15] he finally reaches the answer and the hope in death: 'There is also, whatever it means, the resurrection of the body. We cannot understand. The best is perhaps what we understand least'.[16] As for C.S. Lewis so for us. All of our life is a preparation for this final certainty, although we might not yet know exactly what this certainty means. While we may *feel* the silence and apparent absence of God, the victory *is* won. We may not understand but we are told to rest assured of the ultimate mystery that is presently glimpsed only through a veil. A mystery grounded in a confidence of an assurance that God will wipe away every tear.

So we have looked at what growing old and dying means for us as individuals. But the next question we need to answer is how do we act with this knowledge? How do we cooperate with God in society, among a world of people, many of whom are in old age, all of whom will at some time pass through the stage of dying. And it is here we see the importance of a clear theology. For theology is no mere academic argument. It is not only the basis for our individual faith, but it is the foundation for our relationship with God and so the reason for our practical actions. We are the way God works in the world today.

The Practical Response to Ageing and Dying: The Tradition of Christian Care

The Christian's responsibility then, in bringing God's healing and wholeness to the ageing and dying, whether Christian believers or not, lies in the message of hope brought through the practicality of sacrificial caring. The moral imperative is *agape* (self-giving love). As Hebblethwaite writes:

> The subject matter of Christian ethics is human goodness and human community, as the lives of men and women are conformed to Christ through the working of his Spirit. The proof of the theory lies in the practice. A study of the practical adequacy of Christian ethics would be a study of actual Christian lives, of saints and social reformers, of men and women who have shown the love of Christ in their protest at injustice, and in caring for the poor, the sick and dying, often in situations of utter hopelessness, at least by any purely human standard.[17]

Yet, before examining this response it should be emphasized that the response of care, because it originates from the foundation of creation and covenant, does not hold to a passive acceptance of disease, ageing and dying. As the historian Keith Thomas has argued,[18] it was precisely Christian religious principles that, in the west, led to the decline of pagan superstition in the Middle Ages and laid the groundwork for scientific medicine to develop. This contrasts with the situation in the eastern countries, described by Garlick,[19] where there is a more passive acceptance of suffering and dying, with the result that scientific medicine is seen as an interference with the inevitable laws of nature. The Judeo-Christian tradition, in which the transcendent God is both Creator and Redeemer, and for whom wholeness is both material and spiritual, teaches that natural science is a means of cooperating with the Creator in preventing and overcoming disease and so postponing death. As Midgely[20] observes, this tradition asserts the basic goodness of the world. It is summed up by the doctrine of *imago dei* (the image of God in humans).[21]

Historically, the gospel message of love for one's neighbour introduced a new compassion for the sick at a time when Greek medicine was generally scientific and intellectual rather than com-passionate. This new ethic ushered in by Christ, expounded in the Sermon on the Mount and exemplified in the parable of the Good Samaritan, proclaimed a new understanding of love, *agape*, that revolutionized the care of the sick and dying in the pre-modern world.[22] Lord Walton of Detchant, in his 1990 Harveian Oration, given at the Royal College of Physicians, emphasizes that the Greeks concentrated firstly on *philia* with its understanding of humanity in the abstract, and secondly, the love of the art of medicine. In this Hippocratic tradition differential treatment was given to the rich, to the poor and to slaves, and it was considered unethical to treat a patient with a deadly disease, for this challenged nature and the gods. The Christian ethic of *agape* was a profound change, for it concentrated on *anthropos* rather than *technie*. This is clearly described in Harnack's seminal historical examination of the early church. Harnack quotes bishop Dionysius' account of the different attitudes to the sick and dying among pagans and Christians in response to the plague that raged in Alexandria in 259 AD.

> The most of our brethren did not spare themselves, so great was their brotherly affection. They held fast to each other, visited the sick without fear, ministered to them assiduously, and served them for the sake of Christ. Right gladly did they perish with them . . . Indeed many did die, after caring for the sick and giving health to others, transplanting the death of others, as it were, into themselves. In this way the noblest of our brethren died, including some presbyters and deacons and people of the highest reputation . . . Quite the reverse was it with the heathen. They abandoned those who began to sicken, fled from their dearest friends, threw out their sick when half-dead into the streets, and let the dead lie unburied.[23]

Troeltsch has shown that it was this same spirit that motivated the care of the sick and dying in the Middle Ages.[24] Christian charity was performed by religious orders, but it would be mistaken to believe that in the post-Reformation period the dissolution of the monasteries, and thus religious orders, automatically resulted in a diminishing of the care for the sick. Rather, it became the responsibility of the Christianized society, and as Jordan's social history has shown, this spirit of charity led to the founding of hospitals for those who could not be cared for at home.[25]

Yet, as Troeltsch shows, it was when this Christian spirit weakened that the works of mercy, and thus the care of the sick and dying, were affected, whether in Protestant or Catholic countries. This is clearly illustrated by the writings of Vincent de Paul.[26] He found the care of the sick badly neglected in his contemporary seventeenth-century France and his response was to found an order of nursing nuns, the Sisters of Charity. In England, as Weber has argued, the eighteenth-century Enlightenment saw a gradual weakening of the Christian spirit. According to Tonnies community was replaced by institution, *Gemeinschaft* by *Gesellschaft*, and the care of the sick was delegated contractually to paid servants with a consequent diminishing in the quality of care.[27] Nightingale wrote in 1851: 'Where women undertake so toilsome an office, for hire, and not for love, it cannot be otherwise.'[28] Thus it was that at the outbreak of the Crimea, *The Times* looked enviously to the care given to wounded soldiers by the Sisters of Charity and bemoaned the lack of a similar quality of nurse in England.[29]

The spirit of *agape, caritas*, charity, was thus the driving force for the care of the sick and dying. This was the founding principle for the Lutheran Pietist, Pastor Fliedner's order of deaconesses at Kaiserswerth near Dusseldorf in the 1830s, the work of which Cicely Saunders describes with reference to Worcester's 1935 classic *The Care of the Aged, the Dying and the Dead* as 'caring for the dying more beautifully "than anywhere else in the world"'.[30] And it was at Kaiserswerth that Nightingale first sought to fulfil her vocation and answer the call of God to improve care for the sick and dying. She wrote after her return from Kaiserswerth:

For every want we can always find a divine supply. And accordingly, we see, in the very first times of Christianity, an apostolical institution for the employment of woman's powers directly in the service of God. We find them engaged as 'servants of the Church'. We read, in the Epistle to the Romans, of a 'Deaconess,' as in the Acts of the Apostles, of 'Deacons.' Not only men were employed in the service of the sick and poor, but also women . . . 'Many chose,' it is said, 'the single state, not because they expected thereby to reach a super-eminent degree of holiness, but that they might be better able to care for the sick and the young.[31]

Nightingale had a complex theology but a clear faith, influenced by an evangelical mother and a Unitarian father; her writings and letters clearly reflect her profound biblical beliefs. The care of the sick is a gift to God, and the life of a nurse the life of prayer. The 'good nurse should be "the Sermon on the Mount" in herself'.[32] Nightingale's tremendous influence in reviving the conception of caring as a Christian vocation cannot be underestimated. Her work in the Crimea and later in founding the Nightingale School at St Thomas' bears witness to her belief that the Christian response to sickness and dying lay in an approach that grounded scientific medicine in loving care. During her work in the Crimea, described by her biographers, Cook[33] and Woodham-Smith,[34] Nightingale believed that helping soldiers write letters home was as much part of the nurse's care as attending to his physical needs. Moreover she never allowed a soldier to die alone.

In her annual address to the probationers at the Nightingale School, Nightingale wrote of the wholeness of the nurse's care, its spiritual dimension and heart, and warned of the diminishing of its underlying inspiration:

. . . how shallow a thing is Hospital life – which is, or ought to be, the most inspiring – without deep religious purpose! For, as years go on, we shall have others to train; and find that the springs of religion are dried up within ourselves. The patients we shall always have with us while we are Nurses. And we shall find that we have no religious gift or influence with them – no word in season whether for those who are to live, or for those who are to die – no, not even when they are in their last hours, and perhaps no one by but *us* to speak a word to point them to the Eternal Father and Saviour; not even for a poor little dying child, who cries: 'Nursey, tell me, oh, why is it so dark?'.[35]

This spiritual motivation then undergirded the history and tradition of care for the weak and vulnerable through the faithful action of the believing community, the Church. Evelyn Pearce, an examiner for State Registration of Nurses, and the writer of the classic nursing textbook *A General Textbook of Nursing* that by 1967 had reached seventeen editions, expressed the same spirit of 'total patient care' particularly in her chapter on the care of the dying. But it seems that throughout the twentieth century the spiritual motivation of *agape* in nursing care became subordinated to the increasingly scientistic emphasis on cure, a movement that worried many eminent nurses, for example, Fox, the Matron of The Prince of Wales' Hospital, Tottenham[36] and MacManus, Matron of Guy's.[37] Nightingale had warned against this professionalization, and it was the substance of her bitter disagreement with Bedford Fenwick. For she foresaw that a purely scientific nurse was in danger of becoming a heartless nurse if the spiritual ethic, the moral framework of care, was allowed to diminish. Nightingale's fear was justified, for Pearce, in the 1950s, was motivated to write a small book that explicitly restated the Christian underpinning care.[38] She felt this could no longer be left implicit, as she seemed to assume in her textbook, but in an increasingly technological age it needed to be reiterated. Despite her efforts however, nursing theory from the 1970s onward has become influenced by North America and particularly sociological, psychological and educationist theory. This together with a debunking of the tradition has increasingly marginalized the Christian ethic of care. To use Berkhof's analogy, the gospel fruit has been picked while the gospel tree has been destroyed.[39]

Care for the Dying

Pearce's textbook describes the care of the ageing and dying and her approach demonstrates the same principles that underpinned the vision of Cicely Saunders in the Hospice Movement. Pearce suggests that as the doctor withdraws from the dying person, so the nurse's presence to console and comfort the patient is increasingly important and she is definite that: 'No-one should ever be allowed to die alone'.[40] Pearce stresses the physical aspects of such care, holding the hand, wiping the eyes, moistening the lips, helping the patient relieve his bladder, speaking words of comfort even if the patient is unconscious and apparently unperceiving. But she also stresses the importance of the supernatural effects of prayer and the sacraments for those who are believers, which remove 'trouble and anxiety' and establish 'peace, trust, confidence and acceptance. Many of the prayers are for a return of health and strength, if this be God's will'. And as she continues, 'The nurse will appreciate the deep consolation brought to the heart of her patient by reception of the sacraments which to him are channels instituted by Christ through which His grace flows'.[41]

The Hospice Movement

According to her biographer, du Boulay, in the 1950s Cicely Saunders sought to translate her own Christian commitment into better care for the dying.[42] From her own personal experience with a dying patient, it seems that Saunders found, like Pearce, that increasingly technological care was ignoring the needs of those who could not be cured, the dying. Her inspiration was to found both a Christian and medical foundation that used the most up-to-date scientific advances in symptom control, but grounded in a firm Christian foundation of care. This was strengthened by her experience at both the Methodist home for the dying poor, St Luke's, and St Joseph's Hospice, Hackney, a Roman Catholic foundation, run by the Irish Sisters of Charity, its motto, *Caritas Christi urget nos.* As Saunders writes, she was impressed by the loving care of the dying provided by the nuns.[43] Interestingly, each of these homes for dying people were underpinned by the same biblical text taken from Matthew 25: 'I was sick and you visited me'.[44]

Saunders is explicit that St Christopher's was a response to God's call: 'We believed that in this response we would learn to be the instruments of His care for the suffering and bereaved, and show our patients and their families the care by deeds rather than words which would help them into a healing relationship with Him and also encourage new skill and attitudes far more widely.'[45] Here then is the response of the Christian community, through the inspiration of an individual leader, to bring the Church's ministry of healing to the dying and their families, not primarily by words but through the action and activity of love.

Saunders enshrined these principles in the statement of St Christopher's aims and basis which was prepared together with the theologian, Dr Olive Wyon, in 1961–65 and which by 1988 had remained virtually unchanged. Here the principles of love, freedom and community are reiterated and it is stressed that people must be free from any kind of proselytizing pressure. And the statement concludes with a definite assertion that the organization must rest on the firm foundation of faith which is its security and hope for those who are dying, and also, importantly, the strength and peace for those who are caring:

> That to be of any real use such a Foundation must give the patients – whether they have faith or not – a sense of *security*: through faith in God, through Christ's victory over pain and death, through mutual fellowship, and the spirit of prayer, radiating out from the Chapel into every part of the corporate life.[46]

We have suggested that the theology of our care for those who are dying rests on the grace of God and that this has been both historically and doctrinally its strength and its inspiration. And it may be emphasized here that this theology of care holds at its centre the absolute freedom of the cared-for. There can be no question of imposing ideology on vulnerable people, but only of offering freedom, love and space to all those in need, irrespective of culture, creed or religion. So we may suggest that the work of the hospice movement in caring for the dying should now be extended to those who are living with the effects of chronic ageing and who are often marginalized in our current health care system. Yet, we also need to realize that the hospice movement itself has changed as its spiritual inspiration has weakened.

The Secularization of Care for the Dying

The hospice ideal has now become susceptible to the forces of secularization with implications for the care of the dying. Drawing on Max Weber's sociological thesis, Field[47] and James and Field[48] have pointed to the institutionalization and bureaucratization of hospices. According to Field, this process occurs 'once the dedicated and "charismatic" idealists who were responsible for their foundation and the first cadre of highly selected staff leave'.[49] Unfortunately Field and James do not articulate or analyse the basis of this charisma but rather vaguely state that religion in general and Christianity in particular gave the impetus to the hospice movement. They are thus unable to determine either the implications of theological principles in the care of the dying or the significance of their being neglected and undermined. But Weber himself did analyse the relation between religious faith and practice, and as he pointed out the charismatic leader is inspired by a deep sense of vocation and so views service as a response to the call of God.[50] As he argued, it is through the processes of secularization that this original spiritual inspiration becomes attenuated.

From a Weberian perspective it clearly becomes inevitable that when hospices, and care for the dying generally, lose the spiritual dimension which is their underpinning, the fruit of a gospel faith, so they lose what Field calls their 'specialness'.[51] Indeed, according to O'Donovan, Professor of Moral Theology at Oxford, this loss opens up care for the dying to secular forces and he warns that palliative care may then become a technique through which professionals can soulessly exercise power.[52] But this is precisely Berkhof's point that the gospel fruits are taken from the gospel tree. If the gospel tree is not protected and supported by the people of faith, both visibly and audibly, then the fruit will eventually no longer be produced, and a very different tree will grow.

Bell believes that the North American Hospice Movement, in taking the concept of hospice care without its spiritual foundations, has become subject to both reductivism and atomization. He suggests that in treading the delicate path between the twin dangers of proselytizing and imposing ideology on vulnerable people on the one hand, and of taking a position of passivity akin to emptiness on the other hand, the hospice movement has adopted an ethos of a 'watered down humanistic psycho-dynamic pabulum'.[53] Bell's analysis is supported by a conference in North America in 1986 which sought to define the spiritual component of care for the terminally ill felt to be missing from the North American Hospice Movement. From among the participants, who held Christian, Jewish, Buddhist, humanistic and atheistic viewpoints, it was the Jewish rabbi and Jewish medical director who both suggested that the Christian attitude to dying and particularly the hope of resurrection offer a unique basis for the care of the dying. As the medical director comments to the Christian chaplain:

I'm really struck by your last sentence. The resurrection as a cornerstone, as a foundation is so important to you, sometimes

I find myself wishing I could believe that because it feels so helpful. If I, as a reasonably religious person, envy someone who has a religious belief, how much more must a person who is merely a humanist feel.[54]

The Church's Response to the Secularizaton of Care for the Dying

The question, then, is how should Christians respond? Does it matter if the gospel fruit of hospice is taken away from the gospel tree? Are the clear originating Judeo-Christian principles *really* needed to underpin the concept and practice of hospice care for the dying, or are human feelings and secular, anthropocentric beliefs and values an adequate, even preferable replacement and basis for the future development of care for the ageing and dying? This is the issue which now confronts Christians, whether we are actively involved in care, or whether we support others who are. As the whole Church of God we need to make our voice heard in the debate of the future developments and direction of care for the sick and dying in our society. This is a debate that we ought not ignore or be reluctant to enter into, for it can be argued, both historically and philosophically, that when the spiritual dimension is marginalized, so both the moral and scientific basis of care is undermined.

Yet of fundamental importance is our theological interpretation and understanding of this spiritual dimension. How and in what manner do we understand the relevance and implications of our faith and beliefs for the framework of holistic care? Christians are themselves divided on theological grounds on this issue. On the one hand, there are those who claim that there is an objective truth upon which to base the care of the dying, a certainty to be held on to amidst all the uncertainty, the unchanging power, strength and assurance at the spiritual heart of care. On the other hand, there is a strong voice from those Christians who claim that the mystery of God for hospice care is a changing experience pre-eminently to be discovered and encountered through the every day inexplicabilities of care.

This latter view was adopted by the working party that was set up in 1989 to examine the impact of hospice experience on the Church's ministry of healing, *Mud and Stars*. The working party found that all the conflicts felt in the group stemmed from the question 'What is God for us today?'.[55] The idea of a transcendent God in the face of suffering was felt by the members of the group to be unhelpful, and indeed, the resurrection was considered to 'prettify' suffering.[56] The working party sought to derive their theology from everyday experience and members thus made objective biblical truths marginal in favour of their 'own truths experienced day by day in clinical and nursing care'. But it leads the writer of the summative chapter to the strange conclusion: 'It is through this every day experience of suffering that we have glimpsed the dark side of God, and cannot in all honesty tame the terror of that experience. God is seen to be very destructive in the working out of his purpose'.[57] This theology shows clear Jungian influence, a gnostic God who is detached, cold and uncaring.

And here we are back with Frances Young. For if we are tempted to play down the biblical truth that God triumphs through the resurrection because we prefer the idea of a God who suffers within creation, we are left with a God who is not sufficiently in charge of his creation: a powerless God. And a God who has limited himself to suffering in creation, mirroring and sharing human experience, leaves the way open for a self-limited God who is unable to care because he has foregone, however willingly, the transcending power of care. And it is just this very quality of transcendence, which the working party are wary of, that makes plausible and possible the expression of anger against God felt by those who are suffering, and deemed so necessary by the working party. As Frances Young, C.S. Lewis and indeed the psalmist show us, we need a God who is strong in his transcendence to cry out against, a God who can take our anger yet remain full of constant and overcoming love. It does not make the anger any less real, but the anger does not resonate in silence, rather it is encompassed by the mystery of a conquering love. Yes, God has identified with Hiroshima, Auschwitz, the young mother dying of cancer and our granny with Alzheimer's disease, but his love reaches beyond. In his compassion and mercy he *does* have the answer for both human evil and human suffering and in time we will know it.

Frances Young's words echo in our minds, for God's nature is love, and love is strength not weakness. Love is able to feel suffering but not be dragged down by it and rendered powerless. Despite everything, as Young has shown, God is able to withstand and transfigure suffering. He is ultimately in charge of his creation and we can trust him. His love is not detached from its creation for the nature of love means that mysteriously he completely identifies with the suffering of humanity within creation. Thus the cross makes no sense without the resurrection, just as the resurrection makes no sense without the cross. Both events reveal the nature of love as two sides of the one coin of compassion, inextricably linked as the character and person of our constant and unchanging God.

Thus while *Mud and Stars* points to human experience to claim that there are no neat answers, biblical theology teaches that the answer cannot be derived from the subjectivity of human experience alone but needs to be grounded in the truth of faith through the objectively revealed word of God. There is a fundamental clarity about the gospel which has clear and certain implications for both our own personal relationship with God throughout our lives, as well as our relationship with our fellow human beings. So our theology, our understanding of the way God relates to human beings, is no mere academic exercise, but the soil which both roots, nourishes and sustains our faith and our hope, our attitudes and our actions in our perishable world of growing old and dying.

As Christians we need to hold on to a clear biblical message to provide us with a foundation for us as individuals in our own personal journey as we grow old and die; and as members of the community of the universal Church, as we respond to those in need, as we are called to care. This call or vocation is very costly for it demands a commitment both from the individual and from the community that is long-term and ongoing. It is an action of prayer in the community of faith that involves the whole of the person and the whole of the community in building and sustaining relationships with those who are suffering, ageing and dying, for however long they are required. Furthermore, such relationships do not depend on the capriciousness of human feelings, to be made with those people who respond or who are particularly appreciative. Rather it is for anyone in need, whatever their personal attributes, personal beliefs or personal responsibility. This is ultimately the Church's ministry of healing, its demonstration of the love of God, the self-giving love of the Christian community to whoever is in need, and this is the ultimate test of Christian faith.

The strength for such care depends not on human capabilities, for how can I genuinely understand and so share the sufferings of another however hard I might try? Rather it is to be found in the confidence of Jesus Christ. The truth of the resurrection is not a mere future hope, but the promise of re-creation and regeneration for the present, the here and now, as taught in 2 Corinthians 5 and 1 Corinthians 15. This is the strength on which *agape* rests, and it is the power and security of care for those who face ageing and dying and for those who care for them. Without this hope in the power of regenerating love, care itself is open to a passivity and futility in the face of insurmountable forces. Dying and rising is the very way of caring, the way of self-giving love, and it is the promise of healing that God offers to all humanity through the response of Christian men and women, inspired by the Holy Spirit and conformed to his image and likeness. This is our strength and our hope.

When the perishable puts on the imperishable, and the mortal puts on immortality, then shall come to pass the saying that is written: 'Death is swallowed up in victory.'

(1 Corinthians 15.54)

References

1. Quoted by S. Clark, *A Parliament of Souls* (Clarendon Press 1990), p. 117.

2. A. Comfort in J. Roslansky, ed., *The End of Life: A Discussion at the Nobel Conference* (North-Holland Publishing Company 1973), pp. 51–52.

3. Quoted in V. Carver and P. Liddiard, *An Ageing Population* (Hodder & Stoughton 1978), p. ix.

4. F. Nietzsche, *Twilight of the Idols/The Antichrist*, tr. R. Hollindale (Penguin 1968), p. 88.

5. J. Casson, *Dying: The Greatest Adventure of My Life* (Christian Medical Fellowship 1980), p. 6.

6. S. Weil , *The Need for Roots*, tr. A. Willis (Routledge & Kegan Paul 1987), p. 286.

7. P. Fiddes *The Creative Suffering of God* (Oxford University Press 1988), p. 173.

8. Fiddes, *The Creative Suffering of God*, p. 173..

9. F. Young, *Face to Face* (T and T Clark 1990), p. 237.

10. Young, *Face to Face*, p. 238.

11. Young, *Face to Face*, p. 239.

12. K. Barth, *Church Dogmatics* (T and T Clark 1960), III/2, p. 596.

13. J. Charley, *50 Key Words to the Bible* (Lutterworth 1971), p. 42.

14. C. S. Lewis, *The Problem of Pain* (Fontana 1957).

15. C. S. Lewis, *A Grief Observed* (Faber & Faber 1966), p. 27.

16. Lewis, *A Grief Observed*, p. 59.

17. B. Hebblethwaite, *The Adequacy of Christian Ethics* (Marshall, Morgan & Scott 1981), p. 135.

18. K. Thomas, *Religion and the Decline of Magic* (Penguin 1971).

19. P. Garlick, *The Wholeness of Man* (The Highway Press 1943).

20. M. Midgely, *Wickedness* (Routledge 1984).

21. D. Cairns, *The Image of God in Man* (Fontana 1973).

22. A. Richardson, ed., *A Dictionary of Christian Theology* (SCM 1969), article on 'Love'.

23. A. Harnack, *The Mission and Expansion of Christianity in the First Three Centuries* (Harper Torchbooks 1961), pp. 171–172.

24. E. Troeltsch, *The Social Teaching of the Christian Churches* (George Allen & Unwin 1931), vols. 1 and 2.

25. W. K. Jordan, *Philanthropy in England 1480–1660* (George Allen & Unwin, 1959).

26. Quoted in R. Wilson, *The Life of Vincent de Paul* (Rivingtons 1873).

27. F. Tonnies, *Community and Association* (tr. C. Loomis) (Routledge & Kegan Paul 1955).

28. F. Nightingale, *The Institution of Kaiserwerth on the Rhine for the Practical Training of Deaconesses under the Direction of the Rev. Pastor Fleidner* (The London Ragged Colonial Training School 1851), p. 15.

29. C. Woodham-Smith, *Florence Nightingale* (Penguin 1955).

30. C. Saunders, 'The Modern Hospice', in F. Wald, ed., *In Quest of the Spiritual Component of Care for the Terminally Ill* (Yale University Press 1986), p. 41.

31. Nightingale, *The Institution of Kaiserwerth*, pp. 8–9.

32. F. Nightingale, 'Nursing the Sick', in R. Quain, ed., *A Dictionary of Medicine* (Longmans, Green & Co., 1882), Part II, p. 1048.

33. E. Cook, *The Life of Florence Nightingale* (Macmillan & Co. 1913).

34. Woodham-Smith, *Florence Nightingale*.

35. F. Nightingale, (1873), Letters and addresses to the Probationer Nurses in the 'Nightingale Fund' School at St Thomas's Hospital and Nurses who were formerly trained there. Original letters and Prints for private circulation held by University College, London, p. 3.

36. M. Fox, 'Nursing Ethics', *Nursing Times*, 8.366 (1912), pp. 475–478.

37. E. MacManus, *Matron of Guy's* (Andrew Melrose 1956).

38. E. Pearce, *Nurse and Patient* (Faber & Faber 1969), third edition.

39. H. Berkhof, *An Introduction to the Study of the Christian Faith* (Eerdmans 1979).

40. E. Pearce, *A General Textbook of Nursing* (Faber & Faber 1967), seventeenth edition, p. 718.

41. Pearce, *A General Textbook of Nursing*, pp. 718–719.

42. S. du Boulay, *Cicely Saunders* (Hodder & Stoughton 1984).

43. C. Saunders, 'Working at St Joseph's Hospice', *Annual Report of St Vincent's Hospital* (Dublin 1962).

44. C. Saunders, 'I Was Sick And You Visited Me', *Christian Nurse International*, 3.4 (1987), pp. 4–5.

45. Saunders, 'The Modern Hospice', p. 42.

46. *Aims and Basis Statement,* St Christoper's Hospice, Sydenham, London, 1988.

47. D. Field, *Nursing the Dying* (Tavistock/Routledge 1989).

48. N. James and D. Field 'The Routinization of Hospice: Charisma and Bureaucratization', *Soc.Sci.Med.*, 34.12 (1992), pp. 1363–75.

49. Field, *Nursing the Dying*

50. M. Weber, *Essays in Sociology*, H. Gerth, C. Wright Mills, eds., with new preface by B. Turner (Routledge 1991).

51. Field, *Nursing the Dying*.

52. O. O'Donovan, quoted in R. Twycross, *A Time to Die* (Christian Medical Fellowship 1984), p. 15.

53. H. Bell, 'The Spiritual Care Component of Palliative Care', *Seminars in Oncology*, 12.4 (1985), p. 483.

54. S. Klagsbrun, 'Comments' in Wald, *In Quest of the Spiritual Component*, p. 117.

55. Working Party, *Mud and Stars*, (Sobell Publications 1991), p. 232.

56. Working Party, *Mud and Stars*, p. 225.

57. Working Party, *Mud and Stars*, p. 233.

APPENDIX 1

Consensus Statement on the Christian Ministry of Healing

The following statement was prepared during the course of the consultations, its main purpose being to assist in the clarification, the consolidation and the recording of the main points which arose. The text was debated and agreed during the last two of the consultations and through subsequent correspondence. Although there was general agreement regarding the final text, it should not be understood as expressing the precise view of everybody who took part.

What Do We Mean by Health and Healing?

The World Health Organization (WHO) in 1948 adopted a definition of health as 'a state of complete physical, mental and social well-being and not merely the absence of disease or infirmity'. For the Christian these three dimensions are included within the spiritual nature of human beings who were made for relationship with God. The definition then emphasizes the *unity* of the human person (the physical, mental, social and spiritual all interact with each other and with our environment and cannot be treated separately) and the *holistic* nature of health (healthiness involves the mental, social and spiritual as well as the physical and the environmental).

A further dimension of health is that it is not just for the individual but for the family and the wider community. Healthy relationships are vital to both family and community health. In many respects society as a whole is 'sick' and needs to be made healthy.

This holistic view of health is consistent with the biblical picture. In the Old Testament, health is expressed by the word *shalom* (meaning wholeness, completeness, soundness, well-being and harmony – often translated peace). In the New Testament, similar expressions of health are given by Jesus when he said, 'I have come in order that you might have life – life in all its fullness' (John 10.10

GNB) and by Paul writing to the Thessalonians, 'May God himself, the God of peace, make you holy through and through and keep you sound in spirit, soul and body, free from any fault when our Lord Jesus Christ comes' (1 Thessaalonians 5.23).

In the world as we experience it, there are clear limitations to the realization of complete health. Limitations to healthiness throughout life occur (sometimes severely) because of in-built genetic defects, the normal process of ageing and the influence of environmental factors as well as through other physical or mental illness. These limitations also arise from damaged relationships between people or from a weakened relationship with God. The important question we address is the extent to which we can expect some of the limitations to health to be removed through the ministry of healing.

The ministry of healing is often thought of in a restricted sense, but it is important to understand that it includes the practice of medicine (addressing both physical and mental health) with caring and counselling, the call to repentance, the offer of forgiveness and prayer. Forgiveness and restored relationships can be a powerful aid to healing of apparently physical disorders. We emphasize that all of these are God's work. Medicine makes use of what is available in the world God has created; healing through 'medical' means is not to be thought as inferior to healing through other 'spiritual' means. God's will is that in the Christian ministry of healing all available resources should be brought to bear in a comprehensive and complementary manner.

The work of God in the world is characterized by a combination of *nature* and *grace*. The pattern of healing is of *cooperation* between God and his creation, of divine initiative and creaturely response. That cooperation is evident in medical work, in prayer and in caring and spiritual ministry.

Doctors in their work are frequently faced with the unknown. The reasons for illness may not be clear and the response to treatment varies from person to person. The training of doctors tends to lead to a mind-set which excludes the spiritual dimension including the value of prayer. The Christian can bring to medical ministry a clear recognition that it is the work of God, that it needs to be prayerful and that a person's spiritual needs may be related in important ways to his or her physical or mental state.

During the past century the physical health of much of the world has increased dramatically through major improvements in public health provision and through the provision of medical services of all kinds. Much of healing today, especially in the developed world, occurs through the practice of medicine, which increasingly recognizes the need to treat the whole person. Many of the pioneers in medical work have been Christians. There is a lot of potential for improvements, particularly in preventive medicine and especially in developing countries.

Healing in the New Testament

The healing ministry of Jesus was characterized by the wide range of conditions Jesus dealt with (including infections, long-standing conditions or organic disorders, exorcisms, and a few cases of people restored to life), and by the use in most cases of a single word of assurance or command to bring about complete and instantaneous healing. Some healings are identified as important signs authenticating his ministry.

The ministry of Jesus, in which healing was an important part, must be understood in the context of the 'good news of the Kingdom of God', which became a reality in the world with the ministry of Jesus. But Jesus also made it clear that the complete 'coming' of the Kingdom awaits his final coming in glory and the transformation of all creation. For instance, he did not heal all who were sick in Galilee and Judea.

We are living at a time between the two 'comings' of Jesus during which a battle is going on between the kingly rule of God and the powers of evil. Some of the healings of Jesus are described explicitly in terms of freeing people from Satan's power. In other healing stories the compassion of Jesus is emphasized as the driving force behind his ministry. The Church's ministry of healing today can be expected to arise from these same motivations.

Jesus gave the twelve disciples specific authority to heal, as he did when he commissioned the 'seventy' recorded by Luke. Healing is not explicitly mentioned in the accounts of the post-resurrection commissioning by Jesus of his disciples apart from in the second part of the last chapter of Mark's Gospel – a part which is not included in the most reliable early manuscripts.

Healing was part of the ongoing ministry of the early church as recorded in the Acts of the Apostles; among the gifts of the

Holy Spirit mentioned by Paul in 1 Corinthians 12 is 'healings'. However, it is also clear from the epistles that healing is not always to be expected; frequently rather there is an emphasis on God's 'grace being sufficient'. For example, Paul and other members of the apostolic band suffered from several illnesses none of which is said to have been healed miraculously.

In both the Gospels and Acts the presence of faith is a condition, though not a guarantee of healing.

It is difficult in practice to hold together the biblical truths relating to sickness, healing, suffering and death. There is the truth that the body is subject to continual decay along with the material creation and that God's strength is manifest in our weakness. There is also the truth that Jesus, in his compassion, has brought us a fullness of life, a kingdom of God's goodness which he demonstrated as including physical healing. There is no sign of any awkward tension between these two truths in the New Testament either in relation to Jesus' ministry or the life and teaching of St Paul. The early Christian communities lived with both truths without either one denying the other.

The Church's Ministry of Healing Today

A primary aim of the Church's ministry is to bring people into a personal relationship with Jesus Christ; since this enables us to be whole people it promotes healing and health.

There is agreement amongst Christians that healing (through prayer, through medicine and through caring) is an important part of the Church's ministry and that some possess particular gifts in these various areas of healing ministry. God does answer prayer and healing is one of the ways he responds to our needs.

In the Church's ministry over the ages the ministry of healing (through both medicine and prayer) has often been associated with evangelism, as it was in the ministry of Jesus; healing ministry must not be divorced from preaching and evangelism. Healing, by whatever means, must not be overemphasized; a balance needs to be maintained as in the ministry of Jesus.

There is broad agreement that the Church should be involved with health services (especially in care and counsel) and that it should engage in an active prayer ministry (which may include sacramental acts – the laying on of hands, anointing with oil as well as the Eucharist). The practice of healing ministry in the Christian Church differs widely with different amounts of emphasis dependent to a great extent on the degree of expectation.

The main differences amongst Christians regarding healing concern the widely different expectations regarding 'miraculous' physical healing. There is often misreporting and exaggeration regarding 'miraculous' healing. This is dishonouring to God and misleading and unhelpful to others with illness or disease. Some present-day practitioners appear to play up the supposed miraculous nature of the cures, whereas there is no evidence of Jesus doing this, rather the opposite.

Healings having all the characteristics of those in the ministry of Jesus are rare today. Although in the nature of things complete medical histories are not often available, few cases with these characteristics have been documented in western countries in recent years – some would argue that there is no adequately documented case. More cases are reported from missionary situations in countries of the developing world – although they are even more difficult to verify. Why are such Christ-like healings rare today? Some attribute it to a lack of faith on the part of Christians. Others argue that God in his sovereign purposes is just not often working in that way today especially in countries with well-developed health services.

It is appropriate to emphasize the sovereignty of God in the ministry of healing. Some experience healing (by various means), others do not – at least in the way which is requested. It is important that the Church ministers both to those who need healing and to those who are not healed. Especially to be avoided in those who are not healed are feelings of false guilt.

There are powerful spiritual forces of evil present in the world which can cause suffering and block healing. Situations occur when particular deliverance from demonic powers is needed. Scripture (together with psychiatric skill) helps us to identify such particular situations but does not encourage us to attribute directly to particular demons our usual experiences of sin, failure and disease. To do so is confusing and unhelpful.

Suffering: Theological and Pastoral Perspectives

Suffering enters into a wide range of life's experiences. It is not only associated with the physical (sickness or physical pain), but with the mental, the social (e.g. with relationships, loss and bereavement), and the spiritual. Suffering through persecution 'for Christ's sake' is particularly meaningful for Christians.

A view which is both biblical and scientific delineates two aspects of suffering. The first is the pain and suffering associated with the finite, imperfect world (our scientific picture of the world is that capacity for pain and some suffering form an essential part of the fabric of creation). The second aspect is the pain and suffering which results from human sin and the misuse of creaturely freedom.

On the philosophical level of explanation, the omnipotence and love of God can be reconciled with the creation of a world in which evil and suffering are possible because of the actions of free creatures and a risk-taking God. At a more practical level, the question to be answered is not so much 'why does God allow creatures to suffer?' (although the sheer scale of suffering constitutes a real problem), but 'where is God when we suffer?'.

Experiences of suffering play a role, positive or negative, in our development as people, especially in our spiritual development. But because humans are fallen and alienated from God they tend to deprive themselves of the resources available for suffering to be transfigured; instead they endure anxiety, fear and isolation. Our experiences of suffering need to be tempered by the realization of God's involvement in the world's suffering, by the comfort which comes from the promise of final healing and renewal and by the realism which understands that this promise is 'not yet' – it is only to be fulfilled in the future.

Jesus in his life culminating at Calvary experienced not only the 'natural' suffering of created existence but also the 'unnatural' and unjust suffering of fallen creation. Faith in Christ (especially reflection on his cross and resurrection) offers not escape from suffering, but resources with which to pass through the suffering and to transform it from a meaningless to a meaningful experience.

Pastoral perspectives on suffering emphasize the bearing of one another's burdens. This means listening and understanding, patience and compassion. Our own experiences of suffering, of forgiveness and healing, provide much of the basis for our ability to help and comfort other sufferers. Jesus through his work on the cross is the supreme example of a 'wounded healer'.

The pastoral challenge of ministering to the suffering is a daunting task which Christians are not called to bear alone. Our role as servants is to obey God faithfully and then to leave the weight of the task and the outcome to him.

Problems of Mental Health

There is an unfortunate stigma towards the mentally ill in our society, which can be exemplified for religious people by the fear that consulting a doctor for psychological problems indicates a lack of faith. Mental illness tends to affect the most vulnerable in society.

Psychiatry and religion speak different languages. The language of psychiatry is that of symptoms and scientific analysis (which may include scientific descriptions of religious experience and behaviour). The existence of a psychiatric description does not invalidate religious experience; the description of that experience in religious language is complementary to the psychiatric description.

Many psychiatrists are ignorant of the essence of true religion and its benefits. Many Christians are just as ignorant of psychiatry and what it can offer. Psychiatry and Christian counselling both have their limitations in the treatment of mental illness; these can be removed if psychiatrists and counsellors can properly appreciate the value of each other's discipline and work together. There are implications here for training in both disciplines.

Psychiatry often has to address the distortions of religion. Mental illness occurs when 'part takes over the whole', for instance, when obsession with judgement obscures forgiveness or vice versa. It is helpful if such distortions are addressed at both the psychiatric and theological levels.

Psychiatrists can contribute to the understanding and the treatment of those who have become disturbed through involvement in overengineered healing ministries, either because of non-healing or because of the return of symptoms which have been deliberately suppressed by overemotional excitement.

Many people, including sufferers themselves, find mental illness hard to understand and at times frightening. Because of this ignorance there is a danger of overspiritualization. Christians may tend to 'diagnose' some psychiatric disorders as demonic in origin; inappropriate attempts at exorcism can lead to severe consequences.

Growing Old and Dying

Although death is inevitable and may come at any time, in the modern world the tendency is to repress the expectation of death for ourselves and those whom we love. A sense of loss is the common theme in both the process of growing old (loss of physical and mental capability, social status and often financial security) and in the final state of dying (loss of life itself).

If we think about dying we inevitably ask, who am I? The purpose for which we were created in time, in material bodies that grow old and die, is for eternal life with God. As Paul reminds us 'Our outer nature is wasting away; our inner nature is being renewed every day' (2 Corinthians 4.16).

The awful terror, misery and pain of suffering and death are only too real. Of particular concern is the frequent experience of the apparent silence and absence of God. Jesus himself on the cross experienced this, through the loneliness of his suffering and his experience of abandonment and separation from God. But realizing also that, through the resurrection of Jesus, God has triumphed over suffering, we find a God who is strong in his transcendence to cry out against, a God who can take our anger and yet remain full of constant and overcoming love. God is also just; the righteousness of God demands judgement for the depths of human sin, a judgement which implicates us all.

The Christian ethic expounded in the Sermon on the Mount and exemplified in the parable of the Good Samaritan proclaimed a new understanding of love ('agape') that has provided a driving force for, and revolutionized the care of the sick and the dying. The Christian's responsibility in bringing God's healing and wholeness to the ageing and dying, whether Christian believers or not, lies in the message of hope brought through the demonstration of Christian love in the practicalities of sacrificial caring.

As nursing becomes more dominated by technology, there is a danger of it becoming heartless and ignoring the needs of those who cannot be cured. On the other hand nurses are also involved in the move to care in the community where individual care can be provided. Some Christian organizations are developing nursing homes where Christ's love is seen in the practical care of the frail, the elderly and those with dementia. The Christian foundation of care has been the inspiration for the hospice movement and needs to continue to be at its basis. However, here also increasing secularizaton associated with marginalization of the Christian ethos is tending to undermine both the moral and scientific basis of care for the dying.

The suffering of Christ demonstrates to us that God shares our suffering. Through Christ's victory over death in resurrection, death can be transformed. The Christian hope includes the transformation of the material body, 'to be made like to his glorious body' and the looking forward to the new creation in which 'there will be no more death or mourning or crying or pain' (Revelation 21.4).

APPENDIX 2

Participants in the Consultation Process

The occupations, positions and titles given are those held at the time of the consultations

The number in brackets indicates the number of the consultation meetings attended.

Revd Dr David Atkinson, Canon Chancellor, Southwark Cathedral (1)

Dr C.V. Russell Blacker, Consultant Psychiatrist, City Hospital, Truro and Senior Clinical Tutor, Bristol University (2)

Dr Ann Bradshaw, Macmillan Lecturer in Palliative Nursing, National Institute for Nursing, Oxford (3)

Bishop Graham Dow, Bishop of Willesden (4)

Ms Virginia Dunn, Macmillan Clinical Lecturer in Palliative Nursing, National Institute for Nursing, Oxford (1)

Revd Dr Paul Fiddes, Principal of Regents' Park College, University of Oxford (4)

Revd Dr Rex Gardner, Former medical missionary and NHS Consultant Obstetrician (2)

Mr Luke Gormally, Director, The Linacre Centre for Health Care Ethics (1)

Revd Barbara Heather, Minister Swalecliffe Baptist Church, Kent. Former Assistant Chaplain, Burrswood Centre for Christian Healing (3)

Sir John Houghton, Former Director General of the Meteorological Office. Chairman of the Royal Commission on Environmental Pollution (4)

Lady Sheila Houghton (3)

Dr Susan Houghton, General Practitioner (2)

Dr Verna Houghton, General Practitioner. Chairman, Wokingham District Cancer Care Trust (4)

Dr Bill Lees, Former medical missionary, followed by Community Paediatrics, Reading (4)

Dr Barbara Leppard, Consultant Dermatologist, Southampton (1)

Revd Dr Ernest Lucas, Tutor in Biblical Studies, Bristol Baptist College. Formerly a research biochemist (4)

Revd Leonard Lunn, Chaplain, St Christopher's Hospice, London. (Correspondent)

Dr Peter May, General Practitioner (4)

Jean Baroness McFarlane, Former Professor of Nursing, University of Manchester. Ex-President, The Institute of Religion and Medicine (3)

Ven. Trevor Nash, Coordinator, Advisers for Ministry of Healing (ecumenical) – England (4)

Dr Michael Pearson, Head of Department of Theological Studies and Principle Lecturer in Christian Ethics, Newbold College (2)

Mr Michael Poole, Visiting Research Fellow, School of Education, King's College, London (3)

Rt Revd David Pytches, Vicar of St Andrew's Church, Chorleywood, Herts (1)

Mrs Felicity Radford, Acorn Christian Healing Trust (1)

Revd Simon Steer, Associate Director for Education, Christian Impact (1)

Mrs Sheila Smith, Self-employed lecturer and counsellor. Tutor in Counselling, Spurgeon's College, London (4)

Dr Roy Spilling, General Practitioner (4)

Dr Trevor Stammers, General Practitioner and Tutor in General Practice at St George's Medical School (4)

Revd Beaumont Stevenson, Chaplain, The Warneford Hospital, Oxford (1)

Professor Duncan Vere, General physician and church elder. Clinical drug researcher, including study of pain mechanisms (4)

Miss Sarah Whitfield, Director of Consumer and Corporate Affairs, Camden and Islington Health Authority (4)

Revd Dr John Wilkinson, Former medical missionary and consultant in public health medicine (3)

Revd Dr Nigel Wright, Tutor in Theology, Spurgeon's College, London (Correspondent)